ENERGY POLICIES, POLITICS AND PRICES

RESIDENTIAL ENERGY TAX CREDITS

ELEMENTS, ANALYSES AND DESIGN ISSUES

ENERGY POLICIES, POLITICS AND PRICES

Additional books in this series can be found on Nova's website under the Series tab.

Additional e-books in this series can be found on Nova's website under the e-book tab.

ENERGY POLICIES, POLITICS AND PRICES

RESIDENTIAL ENERGY TAX CREDITS

ELEMENTS, ANALYSES AND DESIGN ISSUES

LENA KINGSTON
EDITOR

NOVINKA
New York

For permission to use material from this book please contact us:
Telephone 631-231-7269; Fax 631-231-8175
Web Site: http://www.novapublishers.com

LIBRARY OF CONGRESS CATALOGING-IN-PUBLICATION DATA

ISBN: 978-1-63321-717-1

Published by Nova Science Publishers, Inc. † New York

CONTENTS

PREFACE

Residential energy efficiency can benefit consumers through reduced utility bills, and support national environmental policy objectives by reducing the demand for electricity generated using fossil-fuels and reducing current strains on the electric power grid. Various policies to increase conservation and energy efficiency have been adopted since the 1970s, including tax incentives. Developing and deploying technologies that are consistent with the most efficient use of our nation's energy resources is broadly appealing. This book explores tax credits as a means of promoting residential energy efficiency. It also provides insight on the energy conservation and climate changes.

Chapter 1 – Two tax credits for residential energy efficiency were recently available to taxpayers; one expired at the end of 2013 and under current law cannot be claimed beginning with 2014 tax returns; the other is scheduled to expire at the end of 2016. The expired nonbusiness energy property tax credit (Internal Revenue Code [IRC] §25C) provided homeowners with a tax credit for investments in certain high-efficiency heating, cooling, and water-heating appliances, as well as tax credits for energy-efficient windows and doors. The residential energy efficient property credit (IRC §25D), which provides a 30% tax credit for investments in properties that generate renewable energy, such as solar panels, is scheduled to remain available through 2016.

There are various policy options available for Congress to consider regarding incentives for residential energy efficiency. One option is to let the existing tax incentives expire as scheduled. Another option would be to repeal these tax credits (as proposed in Chairman Camp's tax reform proposal). A third option would be to extend or modify the current tax incentives. Finally, policymakers could replace the current tax credits with a grant or rebate program.

Chapter 2 – The nonbusiness energy property credit is one of a number of federal initiatives that seek to address concerns about U.S. reliance on foreign energy sources and the impact of carbon dioxide (CO2) emissions on the climate. Enacted as part of the Energy Policy Act of 2005, the nonbusiness energy property credit was intended to increase homeowners' investment in energy conserving improvements by reducing their after-tax costs. The credit is calculated as a percentage of qualified spending on such improvements as insulation systems, exterior windows and metal roofs up to a maximum claimable credit. The maximum credit was set at $500 in 2006 and 2007, raised to $1,500 in 2009 and 2010, and lowered back to $500 in 2011.

This report compiles and expands upon information previously presented to Congress in response to congressional request, which asked us to examine factors relating to the nonbusiness energy property credit. To address the request, the authors (1) evaluated factors to consider in deciding whether the credit should be cost-based or performance-based; and (2) estimated how requiring that only spending above a minimum amount be eligible for the credit, or introducing a base amount for the 2009 credit may have affected measures such as the amount of credit claimed, the revenue cost to the federal government, and incentives for taxpayers to increase their spending on energy efficiency improvements.

Chapter 3 – The American Recovery and Reinvestment Act of 2009 (Recovery Act)[1] made important changes to the law relating to energy credits. The Recovery Act modified the provisions for both the Nonbusiness Energy Property Credit and the Residential Energy Efficient Property Credit. The modifications to the Nonbusiness Energy Property Credit were to encourage the purchase of energy efficient property for an individual's principal residence that were designed to reduce heat loss during cold months or heat gain during warm months. The Residential Energy Efficient Property Credit is for use in an individual's principal or secondary residence to encourage the purchase of renewable sources of energy for use in a home. The amount of both of the Residential Energy Credits allowed reduces an individual's taxes owed.

In: Residential Energy Tax Credits
Editor: Lena Kingston

ISBN: 978-1-63321-717-1

Chapter 1

RESIDENTIAL ENERGY TAX CREDITS: OVERVIEW AND ANALYSIS*

Margot L. Crandall-Hollick and Molly F. Sherlock

SUMMARY

Currently, on their 2013 federal income tax return, taxpayers may be able to claim two tax credits for residential energy efficiency: one expired at the end of 2013 and under current law cannot be claimed beginning with 2014 tax returns; the other is scheduled to expire at the end of 2016. The nonbusiness energy property tax credit (Internal Revenue Code [IRC] §25C) provides homeowners with a tax credit for investments in certain high-efficiency heating, cooling, and water-heating appliances, as well as tax credits for energy-efficient windows and doors. For installations made during 2011, 2012, or 2013, the credit rate is 10% of eligible expenses, with a maximum credit amount of $500. The credit available for 2011, 2012, and 2013 was less than what had been available during 2009 and 2010, when taxpayers were allowed a 30% tax credit of up to $1,500 for making energy-efficiency improvements to their homes. The residential energy efficient property credit (IRC §25D), which provides a 30% tax credit for investments in properties that generate

* This is an edited, reformatted and augmented version of a Congressional Research Service publication R42089, prepared for Members and Committees of Congress dated March 18, 2014.

renewable energy, such as solar panels, is scheduled to remain available through 2016.

Advances in energy efficiency have allowed per-capita residential energy use to remain relatively constant since the 1970s, even as demand for energy-using technologies has increased. Experts believe, however, that there is unrealized potential for further residential energy efficiency. One reason investment in these technologies might not be at optimal levels is that certain market failures result in energy prices that are too low. If energy is relatively inexpensive, consumers will not have a strong incentive to purchase a technology that will lower their energy costs. Tax credits are one policy option to potentially encourage consumers to invest in energy-efficiency technologies.

Residential energy-efficiency tax credits were first introduced in the late 1970s, but were allowed to expire in 1985. Tax credits for residential energy efficiency were again enacted as part of the Energy PolicyAct of 2005 (P.L. 109-58). These credits were expanded and extended as part of the American Recovery and Reinvestment Act of 2009 (ARRA; P.L. 111-5). The Section 25C credit was extended, at a reduced rate, and with a reduced cap, through 2011, as part of the Tax Relief, Unemployment Insurance Reauthorization, and Job CreationAct of 2010 (P.L. 111-312). At the end of 2012, the 25C credit was extended for 2012 and 2013 by the American Taxpayer Relief Act (ATRA; P.L. 112-240).

Although the purpose of residential energy-efficiency tax credits is to motivate additional energy-efficiency investment, the amount of the investment resulting from these credits is unclear. Purchasers investing in energy-efficient property for other reasons—for example, concern about the environment—would have invested in such property absent tax incentives, and hence stand to receive a windfall gain from the tax benefit. Further, the fact that the incentive is delivered as a nonrefundable credit limits the provision's ability to motivate investment for low- and middle-income taxpayers with limited tax liability. The administration of residential energy-efficiency tax credits has also had compliance issues, as identified in a recent Treasury Department Inspector General for Tax Administration (TIGTA) report.

There are various policy options available for Congress to consider regarding incentives for residential energy efficiency. One option is to let the existing tax incentives expire as scheduled. Another option would be to repeal these tax credits (as proposed in Chairman Camp's tax reform proposal). A third option would be to extend or modify the current tax incentives. Finally, policymakers could replace the current tax credits with a grant or rebate program—the Home Star Energy Retrofit Act of 2010 (H.R. 5019/S. 3177 in the 111th Congress), for example. Grants or rebates could be made more widely available, and not be limited to taxpayers with tax liability. Enacting a grant or rebate program, however, would have additional budgetary cost.

INTRODUCTION

Residential energy efficiency can benefit consumers through reduced utility bills, and support national environmental policy objectives by reducing the demand for electricity generated using fossil-fuels and reducing current strains on the electric power grid. Various policies to increase conservation and energy efficiency have been adopted since the 1970s, including tax incentives.[1] Developing and deploying technologies that are consistent with the most efficient use of our nation's energy resources is broadly appealing. What remains unclear, however, is what set of policy tools the federal government should employ to meet energy-efficiency objectives.

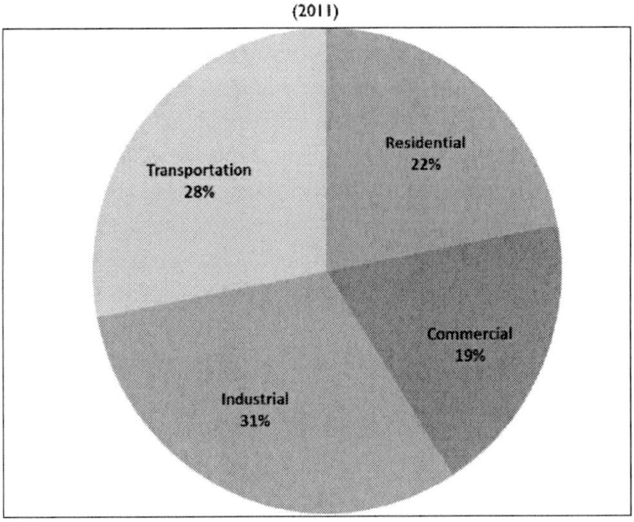

Source: U.S. Energy Information Administration, Annual Energy Review, September 2012.

Notes: Total energy consumption in each end-use sector includes primary energy consumption, electricity retail sales, and electrical system energy losses.

Figure 1. U.S. Energy Consumption by Sector.

(1949–2011)

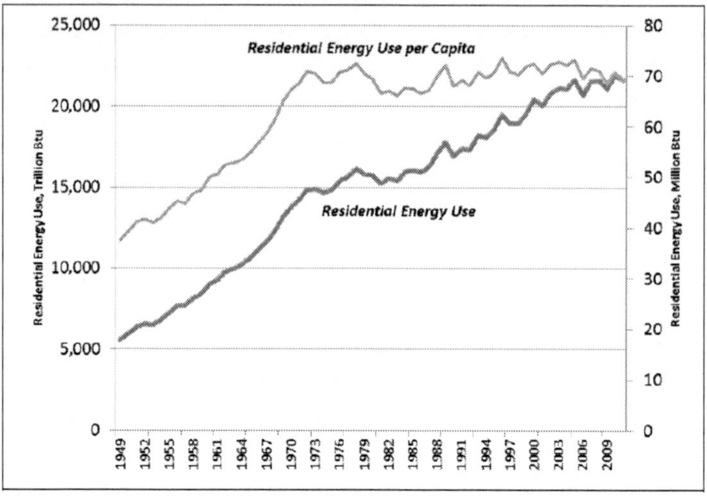

Source: U.S. Energy Information Administration, Annual Energy Review, September 2012.

Figure 2. Residential Energy UseTrends.

In 2011, 22% of total energy consumed in the United States was consumed by the residential sector (see Figure 1). Residential-sector energy use has been increasing over time, with the residential sector today consuming roughly 8% more energy in 2011 than in 2000. Residential energy use per capita, however, has remained relatively constant since the 1970s (see Figure 2). Thus, while overall demand for energy in the residential sector has increased with population growth, efficiency gains have allowed residential energy use per capita to remain relatively flat even as consumers increasingly use energy-demanding technologies.

Although energy-efficiency gains have been made in recent decades, experts suggest that a large potential for increased energy efficiency in the residential sector remains.[2] Despite this potential, concerns remain that consumers may not invest in the optimal level of energy efficiency. If this potential for enhanced energy efficiency is realized in the coming decades, residential energy use trends could change, perhaps leading to reduced residential energy use per capita over time. However, population growth may still result in continued increases in total residential energy use.

This report explores one policy option for promoting residential energy efficiency: tax credits. It begins by providing an overview of the current residential energy-efficiency tax credits[3] (appendices to this report provide a more detailed legislative history). The report then goes on to provide an economic rationale for residential energy-efficiency tax incentives, introducing the concept of "market failures" and "market barriers" which may lead to suboptimal or "economically inefficient" investment in energy-efficiency technologies. That section summarizes various market failures and market barriers in the residential energy sector and outlines ways tax incentives correct them. The final sections of this report provide an economic analysis of the primary tax incentives for residential energy efficiency and briefly review various policy options.

CURRENT LAW

In 2013, taxpayers are eligible to claim tax credits for expenditures related to residential energy-efficiency and residential renewable-energy generation technologies. The first credit, the nonbusiness energy property tax credit (IRC §25C), allows taxpayers to claim a tax credit for energy-efficiency improvements they make to the building envelope (insulation, windows, doors) of their primary residence and for the purchase of high-efficiency heating, cooling, and water-heating appliances they purchase for their primary residence.[4] The amount of the credit is calculated as 10% of expenditures on building envelope improvements plus the cost of each energy-efficient property capped at a specific amount (ranging from $50 to $300), excluding labor and installation costs. Given the price of high-efficiency heating, cooling, and water-heating appliances, taxpayers generally claim the maximum amount of the credit for energy-efficient property. The maximum value of the credit is capped at $500. This cap applies to claims for the Section 25C credit made in the current year, as well as those made in the prior tax year. In other words, if a taxpayer claimed $500 or more of the Section 25C credit prior to 2013, they cannot claim it in 2013. Table 1 summarizes eligibility requirements for residential energy-efficiency tax credits in 2013.

The second credit, the residential energy efficient property tax credit (IRC §25D), allows taxpayers to claim a tax credit for properties that generate renewable energy (e.g., solar panels, geothermal heat pumps, small wind energy, fuel cells) that they install on their residence.[5] The amount of the credit is calculated as 30% of expenditures on technologies that generate renewable energy, including labor and installation costs. The maximum value of the Section 25D credit for renewable-energy-generating technologies other than fuel cells is not capped.[6] The Section 25C credit is scheduled to expire at the end of 2013, whereas the Section 25D credit is scheduled to expire at the end of 2016.[7] For more detailed information on the Section 25C and Section 25D credits, including eligible energy-efficiency property specifications, see Appendix A. A comprehensive legislative history of these credits can be found in Appendix B.

Table 1. Residential Energy-EfficiencyTax Credits in 2014

	Section 25C Credit	**Section 25D Credit**
Calculation of credit	10% of Qualifying Energy-Efficiency Improvements + Qualifying Energy Property	30% of Energy Efficient Property
Types of Qualifying Property	**Qualifying Energy-efficiency Improvements** (1) Insulation (2) Windows (Including Skylights) (3) Doors (4) Qualifying Metal Roof (5) Asphalt Roof with Cooling Granules	**Energy Efficient Property** (1) Solar Electric (2) Solar Water Heating (3) Fuel Cell: $500 per 0.5kW of Capacity (4) Small Wind Energy (5) Geothermal Heat Pumps
	Energy Property and Associated Caps	
	(1) Electric Heat Pump; Central Air Conditioner; Natural Gas, Propane, or Oil Water Heater; Biomass Stove: $300	
	(3) Natural Gas, Propane or Oil Furnace or Hot Water Boiler: $150	
	(4) Advanced Main Air Circulating Fan: $50	
Credit Cap	$200 for windows (lifetime cap)	None
	$500 (lifetime cap)	
Scheduled Expiration	Expired on December 31, 2013	December 31, 2016

Source: CRS analysis of P.L. 109-58, P.L. 109-432, P.L. 110-343, P.L. 111-5 P.L. 111-312, and P.L. 112-240.

THE ECONOMIC RATIONALE FOR RESIDENTIAL ENERGY-EFFICIENCY TAX CREDITS

A rational consumer would be expected to invest in an energy-efficiency technology if the savings that resulted from using the property were greater than the cost of the property. For example, if insulation was expected to lower home-heating costs to such an extent that the homeowner fully recovered the costs of the insulation through lower heating bills, the homeowner would be expected to make this purchase. However, some consumers appear to forgo making these investments, which is known as the "energy-efficiency paradox."

Various economic theories may help explain why consumers do not invest in the optimal amount of residential energy efficiency. Certain "market failures" related to both the production and consumption of energy may help explain why consumers do not make more investments in energy-efficiency technologies, such that the optimal or "economically efficient" number of consumers use these technologies. In addition to these market failures, other market barriers to investment in residential energy efficiency have been identified.[8] The Section 25C and Section 25D credits do not directly correct for some of the market failures and market barriers discussed below, which may limit their impact on increasing energy efficiency.

Market Failures and Market Barriers

There are a variety of reasons why consumers may not make optimal investments in residential energy efficiency. Market failures, including both externalities and principal-agent problems, provide one possible explanation. Other market barriers, including capital market imperfections and informational issues, may also help explain suboptimal investment in residential energy efficiency.

Energy consumption externalities are a potential reason why markets may underallocate resources for residential energy-efficiency investment. Broadly, an externality is a cost or benefit associated with a transaction that is not reflected in market prices. Specifically, residential electricity consumption may be associated with negative environmental externalities, such as pollution costs. If electricity prices do not reflect any potential negative environmental consequences of electricity production, consumers do not pay the full cost associated with consuming electricity. These lower prices lead consumers to consume more electricity than is optimal, and to underinvest in energy efficiency.[9]

Conversely, the adoption of newly developed energy-efficient technologies may result in positive externalities via "knowledge spillover" effects. For example, if one homeowner pays for and installs a new type of solar panel on his home, his neighbors may see this technology, learn about it, and be more likely to adopt it themselves.[10] These knowledge spillover effects mean that, in addition to the benefits to each individual consumer, the adoption of emerging technologies has a greater benefit to society as a whole. Since markets fail to consider the benefits associated with knowledge spillover effects, more of the technology should be adopted than is adopted under the market forces of supply and demand.[11]

Another type of market failure, the principal-agent problem, can occur when there is a disconnect between the incentives for those making energy-efficient property purchasing decisions (the agent) and the ultimate energy consumer (the principal). For example, in non-owner-occupied housing, landlords (agents) may underinvest in energy efficiency when tenants (principals) pay the utility bills.[12] Builders of new homes may also install lower-cost, less efficient technologies if they do not believe the cost of installing high-efficiency products can be recovered when the property is sold. Since the landlord and the builder make decisions regarding the level of energy-efficiency investment, without knowing the energy use patterns of the end user (the tenant or homebuyer), landlords and builders may not invest in the optimal amount of energy efficiency.

Capital market imperfections may also lead households to underinvest in energy-efficiency property. Oftentimes, investments in energy efficiency involve high initial costs, followed by a flow of savings. Purchasers unable to obtain funds up front may purchase less expensive, less efficient alternatives. Low-income households tend to be more credit constrained, and therefore more likely to settle for less energy-efficient alternatives when unable to borrow cash up front.[13]

Finally, when consumers lack information about energy-saving technologies, they may be unaware of the opportunity to make such investments. If consumers have some, but not all the information relevant to make investments in energy-efficiency technologies, they may still be less willing to make these purchases. For example, uncertainty about future energy prices may make consumers reluctant to make irreversible energy-property investments.

How Tax Credits May Address Market Failures and Market Barriers

Various government policies can be used to enhance the functioning of markets in the face of market failures or market barriers. Tax incentives are one option. Other policy options, which are beyond the scope of this report, might include non-tax incentives, such as grants, rebates, or credit enhancements. (Although one particular grant program, Energy Star, is briefly discussed as a policy option at the end of this report, a comprehensive analysis of this policy option is not provided in this report.) The government may also choose to address energy market failures using regulations or mandates. Governments can also support investments in energy efficiency through informational programs (e.g., the Energy Star labeling program).

Policymakers can attempt to correct negative externalities associated with residential energy consumption by using tax credits like the Section 25C and Section 25D credits to lower the cost of energy-efficiency investments, thereby motivating additional investment in these technologies. Other tax incentives not discussed in this report, like the energy-efficient appliance manufacturer credit (IRC §45M), which lowers the cost of producing energy-efficient appliances (known as a "supply-side" incentive), may also bring down the cost of certain technologies. (For a list of residential energy-efficiency tax incentives, see Appendix C, Table C-1.) By encouraging additional investment, the availability of tax credits may also address the positive externalities that result from energy-efficiency technologies in terms of increased awareness about these technologies. Governments can also increase knowledge about technologies with information programs like the Energy Star labeling program.

However, if markets underinvest in energy efficiency because electricity prices are artificially low, tax credits are not the most economically efficient policy option for increasing energy-efficiency investment. Tax credits result in federal revenue losses and can provide windfall gains to taxpayers. The most efficient way to increase investment in energy efficiency under these circumstances would be to allow electricity prices to fully reflect electricity costs. This could be done by removing existing federal financial support for electricity (e.g., energy-related tax subsidies) or by taxing electricity production that generates external costs not currently reflected in market prices. Increasing the price of electricity such that consumers face the full costs associated with electricity consumption would encourage increased investment in energy-efficiency technologies.

Most currently available tax incentives for residential energy efficiency do not directly address the principal-agent problem discussed earlier. The Section 25C and Section 25D credits are not available to renters, and thus do not directly encourage renters to invest in residential energy efficiency. Further, since the Section 25C and Section 25D credits cannot be claimed for investments made to rental property, landlords do not benefit from incentives designed to encourage residential energy-efficiency investments. Other tax incentives not discussed in this report, like the tax credit for energy-efficient new homes (IRC §45L), more directly address potential principal-agent problems in the market for new homes.

Tax credits, which may be claimed several months after eligible purchases are made, will have limited effect in overcoming capital market imperfections for homeowners who may be unable to secure credit to pay for the upfront costs associated with energy-efficient technologies. Although tax incentives for residential energy efficiency do reduce the cost of investment, tax credits may not be the most effective policy option for providing immediate savings to consumers that are credit constrained.[14]

Finally, in cases where consumers lack information about energy efficient technologies, and additional information is not fully effective at alleviating this market failure, policies that subsidize efficiency, like tax credits, may be beneficial and increase the adoption of these technologies, thereby increasing societal welfare. However, recent research suggests that such policies might decrease total welfare if adopted by those who are well-informed about energy efficiency. For such consumers, tax credits will not be necessary to encourage them to make energy efficient investment, and will instead provide a windfall gain to the recipients.[15] Hence, according to this research, tax credits will be of the greatest benefit when they target consumers subject to the largest energy inefficiencies.

Although the two tax credits analyzed in this report are designed to encourage additional investment in residential energy-efficient property in existing homes, they may not rectify other existing market failures, limiting their ability to increase usage of energy-efficient technologies to their optimal or economically efficient levels.

ANALYSIS OF RESIDENTIAL ENERGY TAX CREDITS

The following sections provide a brief economic analysis of the Section 25C and Section 25D tax credits, evaluating their behavioral effects on increasing investment, their fairness or equity, and potential administrative issues. From an economic standpoint, tax incentives are effective if they succeed in causing taxpayers to engage in the desired behavior. In the case of residential energy-efficiency tax benefits, it is not clear how effective such tax credits are at causing additional investment, as opposed to rewarding consumers that would have made investments absent tax incentives. Residential energy tax credits also tend to benefit higher-income taxpayers, an issue which is explored in detail below. Finally, the Treasury Inspector General for Tax Administration (TIGTA) has identified administrative issues with the current tax benefits for residential energy efficiency. The results of their report are also summarized below.

Efficiency: Do Tax Credits Motivate Residential Energy-Efficiency Investments?

The goal of residential energy-efficiency tax credits is to encourage individuals to increase residential energy-efficiency investments. From the government's perspective, these tax policies are successful if tax credits cause additional residential energy-efficiency investment. If, however, tax credits simply reward consumers for investments that would have been made absent such tax incentives, then the tax incentives are not achieving the policy goal. Tax credits that reward consumers for residential energy-efficiency investments, rather than lead consumers to make additional residential energy-efficiency investments, provide a windfall gain to credit recipients without resulting in additional economy-wide energy-efficiency investment or reduced energy consumption.

Concerns that tax credits for residential energy efficiency may not generate additional investment were raised when such credits were first introduced in the 1970s. In 1979, one year after residential energy tax credits were first introduced, several Members of Congress voiced their reservations about these tax credits in a series of House Ways and Means hearings on President Carter's proposals to expand residential energy tax benefits. During one of these hearings, Representative Bill Frenzel remarked,

> I am nervous about tax credits. The principal tax credit bill we passedlast yeardoesnotseem to have given great incentive in the marketplace. The drain on Treasury has been less than we expected because people did not flock to take advantage of it. The tax credit tends

> to be a reward for economic action that was forced by other factors. The tax credit does not motivate, but rather simply occurs at the end of the year when the fellow finds out there was a tax credit available. And I do not think that is a very efficient and effective stimulus.[16]

Empirical evidence evaluating whether the residential energy tax credits available in the late 1970s and early 1980s caused additional investment in energy-efficiency property is mixed. Although some researchers found that tax incentives that reduced the price of energy-efficiency property would lead to additional investment,[17] others found that the tax credits were instead more likely associated with windfall gains to credit recipients as opposed to additional energy-efficiency investment.[18] Whether tax credits can result in additional energy-efficiency investment remains an issue to be considered by policymakers evaluating options for encouraging enhanced residential energy-efficiency investment.

There are several reasons why residential energy tax credits may not have a significant impact on purchasing decisions for many consumers. First, consumers investing in residential energy-efficiency improvements may be responding to other market incentives, such as the high price of energy. For the consumer that would have invested in residential energy-efficiency property without the tax incentive, federal revenue losses associated with the tax credit are windfall gains to the consumer. Second, savings associated with tax credits are not realized until tax returns are filed, often months after energy-efficiency property is purchased. This reduces the incentive power of the credit. Third, tax credits only reduce the price of investment in residential energy-efficiency property for taxpayers having income tax liability to offset with credits. Estimates suggest that in 2011, 46% of U.S. households will have no federal income tax liability, meaning that tax credits for energy-efficiency investment do not provide a current financial incentive for such investments for these taxpayers.[19]

Tax incentives for residential energy efficiency are most likely to motivate energy-efficiency investments for certain types of taxpayers. As noted above, tax incentives only create a financial incentive for investment for taxpayers with tax liability. Thus, higher-income taxpayers are more likely to benefit from residential energy-efficiency tax incentives. Higher-income taxpayers are also more likely to be motivated to invest in residential energy efficiency through tax incentives. Tax credits may also motivate those already in the market for energy property to make more efficient choices. If consumers choose to invest in certain residential energy-efficiency equipment, such as heating and cooling property, only when existing units are no longer operational, tax credits might motivate the purchase of high-efficiency units amongst taxpayers with tax liability.

Equity: Who Benefits from Residential Energy Tax Credits?

The purpose of residential energy-efficiency tax incentives is to increase investment in energy efficiency and properties that generate renewable energy. For these tax credits to be effective, they must be targeted at individuals and households that make choices regarding energy property investments. For residential credits, the target population is homeowners. Taxpayers that are homeowners tend to be higher income than taxpayers living in renter-occupied housing.[20] Hence, it would be expected that energy tax incentives targeted at homeowners would tend to benefit higher-income taxpayers.

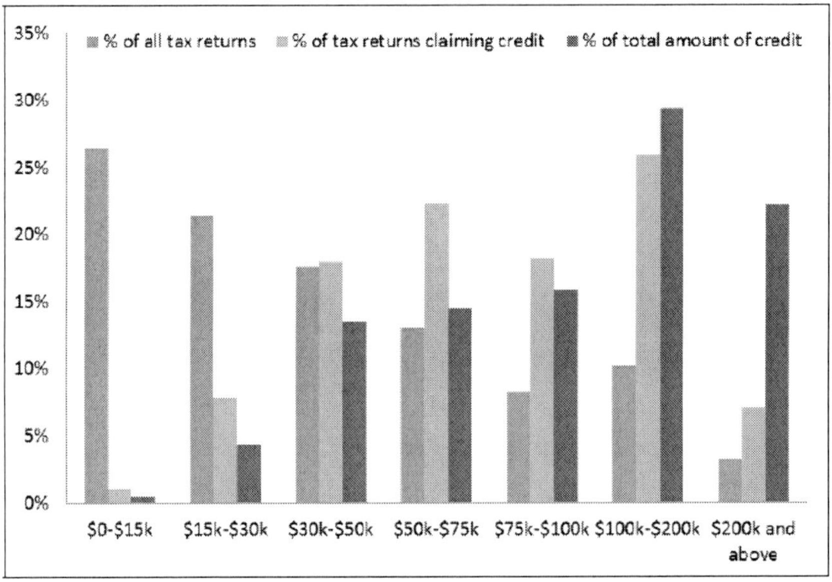

Source: CRS calculations based on the 2011 IRS Statistics of Income (SOI) data, Table 3.3, http://www.irs.gov/ taxstats/indtaxstats/article/0,,id=96981,00.html.

Figure 3. Distribution of the Residential EnergyTax Credits by Claimants and CreditAmount,2011.

Table 2. Distribution and AverageAmount of Residential EnergyTax Credits, byAdjusted Gross Income, 2011

Adjusted Gross Income	Percentage of All Tax Returns	Percentage of Tax Returns Claiming Residential Credits	Percentage of Total Amount of Credit (Revenue Loss)	Average Amount of Credit
$0-$15K	26.5%	1.0%	0.4%	$193.85
$15K-$30K	21.4%	7.8%	4.3%%	$255.82
$30K-$50K	17.5%	17.9%	13.5%	$345.37
$50K-$75K	13.0%	22.2%	14.5%	$299.55
$75K-$100K	8.2%	18.1%	15.8%	$400.99
$100K-$200K	10.2%	25.8%	29.3%	$521.77
$200K and above	3.2%	7.0%	22.2%	$1,454.01
TOTAL	100.0%	100.0%	100.0%	$460.06

Source: CRS calculations based on the 2011 IRS Statistics of Income (SOI) data, Table 3.3, http://www.irs.gov/taxstats/indtaxstats/article/0,,id=96981,00.html.

Note: Items may not sum to 100% due to rounding.

This is borne out in tax data, as residential energy-efficiency tax credits are predominantly claimed by middle-and upper-income taxpayers (see Table 2 and Figure 3). In 2011, roughly three-quarters (73.2%) of residential energy tax credits claims were made on tax returns with adjusted gross income (AGI) above \$50,000.[21] In addition, these tax units claimed 81.7% of the total value of residential credits in 2011.Although tax units with incomes below \$50,000 compose nearly two-thirds (65.4%) of all tax units, approximately one-quarter (26.8%) of tax units in this income class claim residential energy tax credits, claiming less than 19% of the total value of these credits. In addition, as a tax unit's income rises, the average amount of its residential credit also rises, such that tax units with the highest income level receive on average a credit that is more than eight times the average credit value for the lowest income tax unit.

The non-refundability feature of the Section 25C and Section 25D tax credits may limit who can claim these tax benefits. By definition, the value of a nonrefundable credit cannot exceed a taxpayer's tax liability. Although the Section 25D tax credit can be carried forward to offset tax liability in future years, the Section 25C credit cannot be carried forward. Thus, taxpayers without sufficient tax liability in the current year cannot benefit from the Section 25C credit. Taxpayers that eliminate their tax liability through claims of other tax incentives, such as those for the working poor, child-related tax incentives, and education tax benefits, are not able to benefit from certain tax-related residential energy-efficiency incentives.

Residential energy-efficiency tax incentives tend to be limited to higher-income taxpayers which may undermine one of the policy rationales behind using tax credits to motivate energy-efficiency investments. If households are not investing in energy-efficiency property because of the high up-front costs, and because these households are credit constrained, then tax credits that reduce this cost might encourage additional investment. However, if the tax credits are available only to higher-income households, households that are less likely to be credit constrained, then tax incentives may not be the most effective policy option for addressing this market barrier.

Administration: Are Energy-Efficiency Tax Credits Administratively Simple and Transparent?

An ideal tax code would be simple for taxpayers to comply with while also being simple for the government to administer. Taxpayers are more likely to claim tax benefits where compliance costs are low. If filing for certain tax benefits becomes too burdensome, eligible taxpayers might elect not to claim certain tax benefits, and therefore not respond to certain incentives delivered through the tax code.

There may be a trade-off, however, between allowing for tax credits with little reporting requirements and overall taxpayer compliance. InApril 2011, the Treasury Department's Inspector General for Tax Administration (TIGTA) released a report on the residential energy tax credits which found that the processing of these credits provided numerous opportunities for fraud.[22] Specifically, TIGTA found that the IRS could not verify whether individuals that claim either the Section 25C or Section 25D residential credit actually made qualifying energy modifications to their homes and whether the modifications they made were for their residence.

The IRS was unable to confirm that claimants of these credits are eligible for them when income tax returns were processed because they do not require taxpayers to provide information about the residences where they are installed, nor do they require third-party verification (i.e., receipts) that qualifying expenses were incurred. Prior to the issuance of the 2011 tax form (filed in 2012), the form that taxpayers used to claim both of these credits, IRS Form 5695, did not ask taxpayers for any information that would confirm their eligibility for these credits.As a result, TIGTA was unable to confirm that 30% of taxpayers in their sample[23] who claimed the credits were even homeowners. The TIGTA report also noted that analysis of 2009 tax returns indicated that 5% of tax returns claiming these credits did not show any indication of homeownership.

The IRS updated Form 5695 beginning with the 2011 tax year to request additional information about the taxpayer's home where the energy efficiency improvements take place. For example, for the 25C credit, the form now asks taxpayers if the residential energy costs are for the taxpayer's main home in the United States. The form also requests the address of the home where the residential energy efficiency improvements were made, as well as confirmation that the home is an existing (not newly constructed) home. While taxpayers still commit fraud and lie on these forms, this information can be used to determine if taxpayers have mistakenly claimed these credits. TIGTA also found that 362 prisoners or underage individuals were allowed to claim $404,578 worth of these credits erroneously. Generally, prisoners and underage children will be ineligible for these credits because if they are prisoners for an entire year, they will tend to be unable to purchase the energy-saving improvements, and underage individuals are unlikely to have purchased a residence. TIGTA made several recommendations to the IRS, including (1) revise Form 5695 to require the address of the applicable residence and whether that residence was a principal or secondary residence and (2) use available data on prisoners and underage individuals to ensure they are eligible for the residential energy tax credits. Notably, TIGTA did not recommend that the IRS also require third-party validation of qualifying expenditures. Although this information could be valuable in determining eligibility for these credits, it might also increase processing times and costs which would increase complexity for taxpayers and the IRS.

POLICY OPTIONS[24]

The Section 25C and Section 25D tax credits are temporary provisions, and one policy option available to Congress is to allow these tax credits to expire as scheduled. Absent congressional action, the Section 25C credit for nonbusiness energy property will not be available after 2013.

The Section 25D program is not scheduled to expire until the end of 2016. There may be other policy options Congress might want to consider regarding future incentives for residential energy efficiency, including modifying the credits or replacing them with a grant program.

Allow Tax Credits to Expire as Scheduled

One option regarding these credits is to let them expire as scheduled. For taxpayers who base their purchasing decisions on the availability of credits, this may result in taxpayers choosing not to make eligible purchases after their expiration.[25]

However, in so far as the credits are claimed by people who would make qualifying purchases absent these incentives, the expiration of these provisions would eliminate a windfall tax benefit while reducing revenue losses. Under current law, the Section 25D tax credit results in an estimated $0.2 billion in revenue loss annually. The two-year extension of the Section 25C tax credits enacted at the end of 2012 was estimated to result in $2.4 billion in revenue loss between 2013 and 2014.

Extend or Modify Current Tax Incentives

Policymakers may choose to extend, expand, or otherwise modify residential energy-efficiency tax incentives. As detailed in the legislative history in **Appendix B**, the current tax credits for residential energy efficiency have undergone a number of changes since being added to the code in 2005. Extending the credit in its current form, with the $500-per-taxpayer cap in place, would provide limited incentives for additional investment for homeowners that have already claimed tax credits under Section 25C. These credits can be expanded in a variety of ways, including by calculating the credit using a more generous formula, expanding the types of technologies eligible for the credit, and by removing caps (both technology-specific and aggregate caps). Expansions may provide additional incentives that could encourage taxpayers to make more purchases.As illustrated in **Table B-1**, the value of these credits grew nearly five times between 2007 (when both Section 25C and Section 25D were in effect) and 2009 (when ARRA expanded these tax credits). Further, expansion of these credits may also provide additional windfalls to taxpayers who were going to make these purchases anyway.

PROPOSED CHANGES TO RESIDENTIAL ENERGY TAX CREDITS UNDER CHAIRMAN CAMP'S TAX REFORM PLAN

On February 26, 2014, Chairman Camp introduced a draft tax reform bill, which among other tax changes, would repeal both the 25C and 25D tax credits, effective beginning in 2015.

The Joint Committee on Taxation (JCT) estimates that these changes would increase revenues by $2.3 billion between 2014 and 2023, entirely attributable to repealing 25D. Since 25C expired at the end of 2013, repealing it in 2014 would have no budgetary effect.

Policymakers could also scale back these provisions in a variety of ways, including by reinstating technology-specific caps for the Section 25D credit, introducing an overall cap for the Section 25D credit (currently uncapped), reducing the technology-specific caps of Section 25C, or reducing the overall cap on Section 25C. Given that these would be changes from current policy, they may increase confusion among taxpayers when trying to estimate the size of their credits. Policymakers could also phase-out these credits for upper-income taxpayers who would be more likely to make eligible purchases without the credits. Extension of current policy, whether in current form, expanded, or scaled back, will have a greater budgetary cost than expiration of these benefits.

Replace Tax Credits with Grants or Rebates

Finally, policymakers may seek to replace these tax credits with a rebate program, or some alternative mechanism to provide direct cash payments to consumers for eligible purchases. This may be a more beneficial way to provide incentives to consumers purchasing energy-efficiency or renewable-energy-generating technologies, especially for consumers who do not have sufficient funds to make eligible expenditures and cannot wait until they file their taxes to receive a financial benefit from their purchases. Such a program could also benefit those with little or no tax liability who cannot benefit from nonrefundable tax credits. In 2010, both the House and Senate introduced legislation intended to create a rebate program, with rebates payable to contractors installing qualified energy-efficiency property.

The Home Star Energy Retrofit Act of 2010 (H.R. 5019 and S. 3177 and included in S. 3663) would have created a temporary two-tiered rebate program called Home Star. Its Silver Star program tier would have provided up to $3,000 per home in rebates for straightforward home upgrades, including insulation; efficient heating, ventilation, and air conditioning units; new windows; and other measures. The Gold Star program tier would have offered $3,000 rebates for more comprehensive energy retrofits achieving at least 20% energy savings, with rebates increasing up to $8,000 per home for retrofits achieving 45% energy savings.[26] Although some experts believed the Home Star program would result in an increased purchases of energy-efficiency improvements to homes, there were concerns that it could be more costly than expected (the legislation authorized $6 billion in appropriations), that there might be difficulties with its administration, and that it would not provide sufficient benefit to do-it-yourself repairs or improvements.[27] The legislation, which passed the House in 2010, was not considered by the Senate in the 111th Congress. To date, similar legislation has not been introduced in the 113th Congress.

APPENDIX A. SPECIFICATIONS FOR PROPERTY ELIGIBLE FOR RESIDENTIAL ENERGY-EFFICIENCY TAX CREDITS

This appendix provides additional details on the technical standards for property to qualify for the tax credits in IRC Section 25C and Section 25D.

Table A-1.Nonbusiness Energy PropertyTax Credit (§25C) (2012 and 2013)

Property	Qualifying Standard
Energy-efficiency Improvements to Building Envelope	
Insulation materials or systems	Meets 2009 International Energy Conservation Code (IECC) and Amendments
Windows, doors, and skylights	Must be Energy Star Qualified
Roofs	Metal roofs with appropriate pigmented coatings and asphalt roofs with appropriate cooling granules that also meet Energy Star requirements
Energy Efficient Property	
Electric Heat Pump (air source)	For split systems: Heat Seasonal Performance Factor (HSPF)
	≥ 8.5, Energy Efficiency Ratio (EER) ≥ 12.5, Seasonal Energy Efficiency Ratio (SEER) ≥ 15. For package systems: HSPF ≥ 8, EER≥12, SEER ≥ 14
Central Air Conditioner	For split systems: SEER ≥ 16, EER ≥ 13. For package systems: SEER ≥ 14 and EER ≥ 12.
Natural Gas, propane or oil water heater	Energy Factor ≥ 0.82 or a thermal efficiency or at least 90%
Electric Heat Pump Water Heater	Energy Factor ≥ 2.0
Natural gas, propane, or oil furnace	Annual Fuel Utilization Efficiency (AFUE) ≥95
Natural gas, propane or oil water boiler	AFUE ≥ 95
Advanced main air circulating fan: $50	Must use no more than 2% of the furnace's total energy
Biomass Fuel Stoves	Thermal efficiency rating of at least 75%

Source: U.S. Department of Energy, Energy Star Program, http://www.energystar.gov/, *2012 and 2013 Federal Tax Credits for Consumer Energy Efficiency* Updated January 30, 2013.

Notes: In 2012 and 2013, the aggregate amount of credit is limited to \$500 per taxpayer. A taxpayer is ineligible for this tax credit if this credit has already been claimed by the taxpayer in an amount of \$500 in any previous year, including 2009 and 2010 when the aggregate credit limits were higher. The credit is only available for expenditures for an existing home that is the taxpayer's principal residence. New construction and rentals do not qualify.

Table A-2. Residential Energy Efficient PropertyTax Credit (§25D) (2013)

Property	Qualifying Standard
Solar electric and solar water heating property	Qualifying property must be used exclusively for purposes other than heating swimming pools and hot tubs and must meet applicable fire and electrical code requirement. At least half of the energy generated by a solar water heating property must come from the sun and the system must b certified by the Solar Rating and Certification Corporation (SRCC) or a comparable entity endorsed by the government or the state in which the property is installed.
Fuel cell	Efficiency of at least 30% and must have a capacity of at le 0.5 kW
Small wind	Nameplate capacity of not more than 100 kW
Geothermal heat pumps	Water to Air: For closed loop: EER ≥ 17.1 and Coefficient of Performance (COP) ≥ 3.6. For open loop: EER ≥ 21.1 a COP ≥ 4.1.
	Water to Water: For closed loop: EER ≥ 16.1 and Coefficient of Performance (COP) ≥ 3.1. For open loop: EER ≥ 20.1 and COP ≥ 3.5.
	For direct expansion: EER ≥ 16 and COP ≥ 3.6

Source: U.S. Department of Energy, Energy Star Program, http://www.energystar.gov/, *2012 and 2013 Federal Tax Credits for Consumer Energy Efficiency* Accessed March 18, 2014.

Notes: Excluding fuel cell properties, the credit is available for expenditures for principal residences and second homes. Both existing homes and new construction qualifies. Rental units do not qualify. For fuel cell installations, the credit is restricted to principal residences (existing homes and new construction). Rentals and second homes do not qualify.

Appendix B. Legislative History

Tax credits for residential energy efficiency were first introduced in the late 1970s. These incentives were allowed to expire in the mid-1980s. The present-day residential energy tax incentives, introduced in 2005, are similar to the earlier incentives of the late 1970s and early 1980s.

Residential Energy Credits in the 1970s and 1980s

The Energy Tax Act of 1978 (P.L. 95-618) introduced the first tax credit for conservation and renewable-energy generation. Specifically this credit had two components. The first component was calculated as 15% of the first $2,000 of energy-conservation expenditures (a maximum credit value of $300). The second component was calculated as 30% of the first $2,000 in qualified expenditures for solar, wind, and geothermal energy plus 20% of the next $8,000 in qualified expenditures (a maximum credit value of $2,200). The final value of the credit was the sum of these two components, with the maximum value equaling $2,500. In 1980, Congress passed the Crude Oil Windfall Profit Tax Act of 1980 (P.L. 96-223), which increased the amount of the credit.[28] Specifically, this law increased the amount of the second component of the credit attributable to renewable energy generation to 40% of the first $10,000 of expenditures (yielding a maximum value of $4,000 for this component of the credit). This credit was allowed to expire at the end of 1985. Not until 2005, 20 years later, would Congress again enact federal tax credits for residential energy efficiency and renewable-energy property.

The Energy Policy Act of 2005

The Energy PolicyAct of 2005 (EPACT05; P.L. 109-58) created two new temporary tax credits for homeowners who made energy-efficiency improvements to their homes. Under EPACT05, both credits were in effect for 2006 and 2007. The first credit was the nonbusiness energy property credit (IRC §25C). Under Section 25C, taxpayers were eligible for a nonrefundable tax credit equal to 10% of qualified expenditures, subject to certain limitations for specific types of property. Specifically, property-specific credit limits were $50 per year for any advanced main air circulating fan; $250 per year for any qualified natural gas, propane, or oil furnace or hot water boiler; and $300 for electric heat pumps, geothermal heat pumps, central air conditioners, and boilers and water heaters that met certain efficiency standards. The maximum amount of Section 25C credit that could be taken for windows over 2006 and 2007 was capped at $200. The lifetime cap for the Section 25C credit was $500 for 2006 and 2007.[29] The credit could only be applied to improvements made to the taxpayer's principal residence.

The second credit temporary established by EPACT05 for 2006 and 2007 was the residential energy-efficient property credit (IRC §25D). This nonrefundable credit was calculated as 30% of expenditures on qualified photovoltaic properties (where the sun's energy is used to generate electricity), solar water-heating properties (excluding those used for heating swimming pools and hot tubs), and fuel-cell generators, subject to annual limits. Specifically, the credit for photovoltaic and solar water-heating properties could not exceed $2,000 per year, whereas the credit for fuel cells could not exceed $500 per year. Qualifying photovoltaic and solar water-heating property expenditures included those made on any of the taxpayer's residences, whereas qualifying fuel-cell expenditures were limited to those made to the taxpayer's principal residence.

At the end of 2007, Section 25C expired. By contrast Section 25D was extended for the 2008 tax year by the Tax Relief and Health CareAct of 2006 (P.L. 109-432). Further, this act clarified that all property which used solar energy to generate electricity, not just photovoltaic property, could qualify for the Section 25D credit.

The Emergency Economic Stabilization Act (EESA)

In 2008, the Emergency Economic StabilizationAct of 2008 (EESA; P.L. 110-343) reinstated and modified the Section 25C credit for the 2009 tax year. EESAalso expanded the list of qualified energy property to include biomass fuel stoves, which were eligible for a $300 credit. Geothermal heat pumps were removed from the list of eligible property under Section 25C but were added to the list of eligible property under Section 25D.

EESA extended the Section 25D tax credit for eight years, through 2016, modified it for existing technologies, and expanded it to new technologies. Specifically, the act eliminated the $2,000 maximum annual credit limit for qualified solar-electric property expenditures beginning in 2009. In addition, it expanded the credit to include expenditures for qualified small wind-energy property and (as previously mentioned) qualified geothermal heat pump roperty. The credit for qualified small wind energy was equal to 30% of expenditures made by taxpayers on a small wind-energy property up to a cap. The cap was set at $500 for each half kilowatt of electric capacity generated by a wind turbine, not to exceed $4,000 annually. The credit for qualifying geothermal heat pumps was calculated as 30% of expenditures up to a $2,000 annual cap for this technology. Taxpayers were eligible for the credits for both small wind-energy and geothermal properties installed on any of their residential properties.

The American Recovery and Reinvestment Act (ARRA)

TheAmerican Recovery and Reinvestment Act of 2009 (ARRA; P.L. 111-5) further extended and modified the Section 25C and Section 25D tax credits. With respect to the Section 25C credit, ARRA extended the credit for two years (2009 and 2010) and modified the calculation of the credit to be equal to 30% of qualified expenditures for energy-efficiency improvements and energy property, eliminating the technology-specific credit amounts.[30] In addition, the aggregate credit cap was lifted from $500 to $1,500 for 2009 and 2010 and the $200 aggregate cap for windows was eliminated for 2009 and 2010. Hence, if taxpayers used $1,000 of credit in 2009, their credit would be limited to $500 in 2010, irrespective if they had used this credit in 2006 and 2007. The removal of the aggregate cap for windows meant that in 2009 and 2010, taxpayers could claim up to $1,500 in tax credits for qualified windows. Finally,ARRA generally reduced the efficiency standards for both energy-efficiency improvements and energy property, expanding the availability of the credit to additional products.

ARRA also changed the Section 25D tax credit for 2009 and 2010, primarily by removing the maximum credit caps for every type of technology except fuel cells. These changes were effective from 2009 through 2016.

Following the changes made to the Section 25C and Section 25D tax credits under ARRA, the number of credits being claimed and the total dollar amount of credits being claimed increased (see Table B-1). Further, under ARRA, average credit amounts were higher than they had been during 2006 and 2007, reflecting the higher credit rate. When the ARRA expansions expired, the number of taxpayers claiming the residential energy credit fell, along with the total amount and average amount of these credits.

Table B-1. Residential Energy Credits Claimed andAverageAmount, 2006-2010

	Number of Tax Returns Which Include Claims for Residential Credits	Total Amount of Residential Credits Claimed (Millions)	Average Credit Amount
2006	4,344,189	$1,000.15	$230
2007	4,326,398	$1,007.58	$233
2008	225,733	$216.69	$960
2009	6,711,682	$5,822.88	$868
2010	7,155,889	$6,173.49	$863
2011	3,642,988	$1,676.00	$460.06

Source: Internal Revenue Service, Statistics of Income (SOI), Individual Statistical Tables by Size of Adjusted Gross Income, Table 3.3, 2006-2011.

Notes: The Section 25C tax credit expired at the end of 2007 and was unavailable in 2008, hence the 2008 numbers represent claims for the Section 25D tax credit. In 2011, the maximum value of the 25C credit was lowered from $1,500 to $500.

The 2010 Tax Act (P.L. 111-312)

Tax Relief, Unemployment Insurance Reauthorization, and Job Creation Act of 2010 (The 2010 Tax Act; P.L. 111-312) extended the Section 25C credit for one year, through the end of 2011. However, the credit structure returned to the structure that existed prior to the enactment of ARRA.[31] Importantly, the general lifetime limit ($500) and window lifetime limit ($200) were reinstated. Hence, if a taxpayer had claimed a total of $500 in Section 25C credits over 2006, 2007, 2009, and 2010 combined, they would be ineligible for the credit in 2011. Similarly if they had claimed $200 in credits for windows in 2006, 2007, 2009, and 2010 combined, they would be ineligible to claim the credit for windows in 2011. Additionally, certain efficiency standards that were relaxed under ARRA were restored to their prior levels. Finally, the technology-specific credit limits for energy-efficiency property were reinstated at pre-ARRA levels.

The American Taxpayer Relief Act (ATRA)

TheAmerican Taxpayer Relief Act (P.L. 112-240, ATRA) extended the 2011 parameters of the 25C credit for two additional years—2012 and 2013.

Table B-2. Overview of Legislative Changes to the Nonbusiness Energy Property Tax Credit (§25C), 2005-2012

	2005	2008	2009	2010	2012
	P.L. 109-58 (EPACT05)	**P.L. 110-343 (EESA)**	**P.L. 111-5 (ARRA)**	**P.L. 111-312**	**P.L. 112-240**
Calculation of Credit	10% of Qualifying Energy-efficiency Improvements + Qualifying Energy Property (fixed by type. see below)	*	30% of Qualifying Energy-efficiency Improvements + 30% of Qualifying Energy Property (fixed amounts by property type eliminated)	10% of Qualifying Energy-efficiency Improvements + Qualifying Energy Property (capped by type)	*
Types of Qualifying Energy-efficiency Improvements to Building Envelope	(1) Insulation (2) Windows (Including skylights) (3) Doors (4) Qualifying Metal Roof	Added- (1) Asphalt Roof with cooling granules	*	*	*
Types of Qualifying Energy Property and Credit Amount	(1) Energy Efficient Building Property: $300 Electric Heat Pump (air source) Geothermal Heat Pump Central Air Conditioner Natural Gas, Oil or Propane Water heater Electric Heat Pump Water Heater (2) Natural gas, propane, or oil furnace: $150	Added- (1) Biomass fuel stoves: $300 Removed-(2) Geothermal heat pumps	Properties are nchanged, but fixed dollar amounts per property type are eliminated.	(1) Energy Efficient Building Property: $300 Electric Heat Pump (air source) Biomass fuel stoves: $300 Central Air Conditioner Natural Gas, Oil or Propane Water heater Electric Heat Pump Water Heater	*

	2005	2008	2009	2010	2012
	P.L. 109-58 (EPACT05)	**P.L. 110-343 (EESA)**	**P.L. 111-5 (ARRA)**	**P.L. 111-312**	**P.L. 112-240**
	(3) Natural gas, propane or oil water boiler: $150 (4) Advanced main air circulating fan: $50			(2) Natural gas, propane, or oil furnace: $150 (3) Natural gas, propane or oil water boiler: $150 (4) Advanced main air circulating fan: $50	
Aggregate Cap for Windows	$200 over all prior tax years	*	$200 aggregate cap for windows removed for 2009 and 2010	$200 (for all prior tax years beginning in 2006 including 2009 and 2010)	*
Aggregate Cap for Credit	$500 over all prior tax years	*	$1,500 over 2009 and 2010 (excludes expenditures in 2006, 2007)	$500 (for all prior tax years beginning in 2006 including 2009 and 2010)	*
Applicable Tax Years	2006 and 2007	2009	2009 and 2010	2011	2012 and 2013

Source: CRS analysis of P.L. 109-58, P.L. 110-343, P.L. 111-5, P.L. 111-312, and P.L. 112-240.

Note: * Unchanged from prior law.

Table B-3. Overview of Legislative Changes to Residential Energy-Efficient PropertyTax Credit (§25D),2005-2010

	2005	**2006**	**2008**	**2009**
	P.L. 109-58 (EPACT05)	**P.L. 109-432**	**P.L. 110-343 (EESA)**	**P.L. 111-5 (ARRA)**
Calculation of Credit	30% of energy efficient property (subject to maximum credit amount by type of property , see below)	*	*	*
Qualifying Renewable Energy Generating Property and Max Credit Amount by Type of Property *(includes labor costs)*	(1) Solar electric (photovoltaic): $2,000 (2) Solar water heating: $2,000 (3) Fuel Cell: $500 per 0.5kW of power capacity	Clarified that all solar electric, not just photovoltaic property, qualified for the credit,	Added- (1) Small wind energy: $500 per 0.5kW power capacity up to $4,000 (2) Geothermal heat pumps: $2,000 (applicable from 2008-2016) Modified- (1) Solar electric (photovoltaic): max credit amount eliminated	Modified- (1) Small wind energy: max credit value eliminated (2) Geothermal heat pumps: max credit value eliminated (3) Solar water heating: max credit value eliminated
Aggregate Cap for Credit	None	*	*	*
Applicable Tax Years	2006 and 2007	2008	2009-2016	2009-2016

Source: CRS analysis of P.L. 109-58, P.L. 109-432, P.L. 110-343, P.L. 111-5, P.L. 111-312 and P.L. 112-240.

Note: * Unchanged from prior law.

APPENDIX C. BUDGETARY IMPACT OF RESIDENTIAL ENERGY TAX INCENTIVES

Table C-1. Revenue LossesAssociated with Residential Energy-Efficiency Tax Incentives,2008-2017 (billions of dollars)

Provision	2008	2009	2010	2011	2012	2013	2014	2015	2016	2017
Credit for Energy Efficiency Improvements to Existing Homes (IRC §25C)	0.8	0.3	1.7	1.5	2.9	3.0	2.5	-	-	-
Residential Energy Efficient Property Credit (IRC §25D)	-i-	0.1	0.2	0.2	0.8	0.9	1.0	1.0	1.1	0.9
New Energy Efficient Home Credit (IRC §45L)	-i-	-i-	-i-	-i-	-i-	-i-	-i-	-i-	-i-	-i-
Credit for the Production of Energy Efficient Appliances (IRC §45M)	0.1	0.1	0.2	0.2	0.2	0.2	0.1	0.1	-i-	-i-
Exclusion of Energy Conservation Subsidies Provided by Public Utilities (IRC §136)	-i-	-i-	-i-	-i-	-i-	-i-	-i-	-i-	-i-	-i-

Source: Joint Committee on Taxation, JCS-13-1, JCS-1-12, JCS-3-10, JCS-1-10, JCS-2-08

Note: An "-i-" indicates an estimated revenue loss of less than $50 million.

End Notes

[1] Policies that have been adopted to support energy efficiency and conservation, that are beyond the scope of this report, include research and development (R&D) funding, pilot programs, and efficiency standards and mandates.

[2] For example, see Hannah Choi Granade, John Creyts, and Anton Derkach et al., *Unlocking Energy Efficiency in the U.S. Economy*, McKinsey & Company, July 2009, http://www.mckinsey.com/Client_Service/ Electric_Power_and_Natural_Gas/ Latest_ thinking/Unlocking_energy_efficiency_in_the_US_economy.aspx.

[3] The terms "residential energy-efficiency credits" and "residential energy credits" are used interchangeably in this report. The Internal Revenue Service refers to these credits as "residential energy credits."

[4] This residence must be an existing home, not a new home.

[5] For all technologies, except fuel cells, the credit can be claimed for installations of renewable-energy-generating technologies made to any of the taxpayers' residences, not just a principal residence. Eligible fuel cell installation must be made on a taxpayer's primary residence.

[6] The credit for fuel cells is called at $500 per 0.5W of power capacity.

[7] The renewable-energy-generating technology must be placed in service before December 31, 2016.

[8] As part of the Energy Policy Act of 2005 (P.L. 109-58), Congress established an advisory committee to study this issue. In 2007, the advisory committee released a report, *Carbon Lock-In: Barriers to Deploying Climate Change Mitigation Technologies*. An analysis of this report can be found in CRS Report R40670, *Energy Efficiency in Buildings: Critical Barriers and Congressional Policy*, by Paul W. Parfomak, Fred Sissine, and Eric A. Fischer. This report presents market barriers likely to prevent efficient adoption of energy-efficient technologies, drawing on both the *Carbon Lock-In* report and the economics literature on energy-efficient technology adoption.

[9] As an example, consider an individual running an energy-using appliance, such as an air conditioner. While the individual may consider the impact of the air conditioner on their electricity bill, they are unlikely to think about the CO_2 emissions associated with generating the electricity necessary to power the air conditioner. If carbon emissions are not priced, and parties involved in transactions involving carbon emissions do not pay for the environmental cost of such emissions, the market outcome will result in a higher level of emissions than is socially optimal.

[10] Knowledge spillover benefits are most likely to result when consumers are considering adoption of new technologies. Many of the products currently eligible for energy-efficiency tax incentives incorporate technologies that have been available for a number of years, and are thus not new to the market.

[11] Adam B. Jaffe, Richard G. Newell, and Robert N. Stavins, "Technology Policy for Energy and the Environment," in *Innovation Policy and the Economy*, ed. Adam B. Jaffe, Josh Lerner, and Scott Stern, 4th ed. (Cambridge, MA: The MIT Press, 2004), pp. 35-68.

[12] This assumes that landlords are not able to capture the benefits of greater energy efficiency through higher rents.

[13] Low income borrowers that are given loans are likely to face higher interest rates. Since low income individuals face higher interest rates, they are likely to use a higher discount rate when evaluating energy-saving investments. When evaluated using a higher discount rate, fewer projects will appear to have long-run cost savings.

[14] As an alternative, grants or rebates that reduce the cost of energy-efficient property at the time of purchase are a more direct mechanism for reducing upfront costs. If capital market

imperfections are preventing investment in energy-efficient technologies, a consumer loan program would be a more direct option for addressing this market barrier.

[15] For more information, see Hunt Allcott and Michael Greenstone, "Is There An Energy Efficiency Gap?," *NBER Working Paper Series* , January 2012, Working Paper 17766, http://www.nber.org/papers/w17766.pdf?new_window= 1.

[16] U.S. Congress, House Committee on Ways and Means, *The President's Energy Program, Phase III*, committee print, 96th Cong., 1st sess., July 1979, p. 317.

[17] See Kevin A. Hassett and Gilbert E. Metcalf, "Energy Tax Credits and Residential Conservation Investment: Evidence from Panel Data," *Journal of Public Economics*, vol. 57, no. 2 (June 1995), pp. 201-217.

[18] See Michael J. Walsh, "Energy Tax Credits and Housing Improvement," *Energy Economics*, vol. 11, no. 4 (October 1989), pp. 275-284 and Jeffery A. Dubin and Steven E. Henson, "The Distributional Effects of the Federal Energy Tax Act," *Resources and Energy*, vol. 10, no. 3 (1988), pp. 191-212.

[19] See Rachel Johnson, James Nunns, and Jeffrey Rohaly et al., *Why Some Tax Units Pay No Income Tax*, Tax Policy Center: Urban Institute: Brookings Institution, July 2011, http://www.taxpolicycenter.org/UploadedPDF/1001547-Why-No-Income-Tax.pdf; and CRS Report R41362, *Who Doesn't Pay Income Taxes?*, by Thomas L. Hungerford.

[20] According to the American Housing Survey, in 2009 the median income of homeowners was $60,000 compared to $28,400 for renters.[20]

[21] In this section, tax returns and tax units are used interchangeably and include returns with no taxable income. A tax unit is not necessarily an individual, but represents all the individuals included on an income tax return including spouses and dependents.

[22] Treasury Inspector General For Tax Administration, *Processes Were Not Established to Verify Eligibility for Residential Energy Credits*, Reference Number: 2011-41-038, April 19, 2011, http://www.treasury.gov/tigta/ auditreports/2011reports/201141038fr.pdf.

[23] TIGTA examined a statistically representative sample of 150 tax returns.

[24] The policy options discussed here include incentive-oriented options. Alternative policy options could be to impose regulations or standards mandating certain levels of energy efficiency. While standards and mandates may work to increase energy efficiency in newly installed property, imposing standards and mandates provide limited incentives for increasing efficiency in existing residential property.

[25] Alternatively, before the expiration of these provisions, taxpayers may increase their purchases of energy-efficient or renewable-energy-generating technologies to take advantage of these provisions before they expire.

[26] For more information, see http://homestarcoalition.org/HOME_STAR_Overview.pdf.

[27] For more information on the Home Star program, including operational issues, see CRS Report R41273, *The Home Star Energy Retrofit Act of 2010: Operational and Market Considerations*, by Paul W. Parfomak.

[28] For more information on the history of the credit in the late 1970s and early 1980s, see Robert McIntyre, "Lessons for Tax Reformers from the History of the Energy Tax Incentives in the Windfall Profit Tax Act of 1980 ," *The Boston College Law Review*, vol. 22, no. 705 (1981).

[29] In other words, if a taxpayer used $500 worth of §25C credit in 2006 for her home, she would be ineligible for the credit in 2007, irrespective of whether she had qualifying expenses in 2007.

[30] The changes that ARRA made to the §25C credit in 2009 superseded the 2009 changes that had been made to the credit by EESA.

[31] The Section 25C credit in 2011 applies to asphalt roofs with cooling granules and biomass stoves, changes that were made by EESA.

In: Residential Energy Tax Credits
Editor: Lena Kingston
ISBN: 978-1-63321-717-1

Chapter 2

ENERGY CONSERVATION AND CLIMATE CHANGE: FACTORS TO CONSIDER IN THE DESIGN OF THE NONBUSINESS ENERGY PROPERTY CREDIT*

United States Government Accountability Office

ABBREVIATIONS

AGI	adjusted gross income
CO_2	carbon dioxide
DOE	Department of Energy
IRC	Internal Revenue Code
IRS	Internal Revenue Service
SOI	Statistics of Income Database

* This is an edited, reformatted and augmented version of the United States Government Accountability Office publication, GAO-12-318, dated April 2012.

April 2, 2012

The Honorable Max Baucus
Chairman
Committee on Finance
United States Senate

The Honorable Jeff Bingaman
United States Senate

The Honorable Dianne Feinstein
United States Senate

The Honorable John F. Kerry
United States Senate

The Honorable Olympia J. Snowe
United States Senate

The nonbusiness energy property credit[1] is one of a number of federal initiatives that seek to address concerns about U.S. reliance on foreign energy sources and the impact of carbon dioxide (CO_2) emissions on the climate. Enacted as part of the Energy Policy Act of 2005, the nonbusiness energy property credit was intended to increase homeowners' investment in energy conserving improvements by reducing their after-tax costs. The credit is calculated as a percentage of qualified spending on such improvements as insulation systems, exterior windows and metal roofs up to a maximum claimable credit. The maximum credit was set at \$500 in 2006 and 2007, raised to \$1,500 in 2009 and 2010, and lowered back to \$500 in 2011.

In the enclosed slides, this report compiles and expands upon information previously presented to you in response to your request, which asked us to examine factors relating to the nonbusiness energy property credit. To address the request, we (1) evaluated factors to consider in deciding whether the credit should be cost-based or performance-based; and (2) estimated how requiring that only spending above a minimum amount be eligible for the credit, or introducing a base amount for the 2009 credit may have affected measures such as the amount of credit claimed, the revenue cost to the federal government, and incentives for taxpayers to increase their spending on energy efficiency improvements.

Scope and Methodology

For our first objective—to evaluate factors to consider in deciding whether the credit should be cost-based or performance-based—we reviewed relevant literature and consulted with experts on criteria for a well- designed credit. On the basis of this review, we determined that tax credit design, which includes such factors as whether the credit is cost-based or performance-based, should be evaluated according to:

- how well the logic of the design is related to the credit's purpose,
- how likely the design is to achieve that purpose,
- how costly it would be to achieve this purpose using this design, and
- how fairly the credit's costs and benefits are distributed under this design.

Using these criteria, we analyzed the current credit and changes that have been proposed to it.

For our second objective—estimating how introducing a base spending amount for the 2009 credit may have affected measures such as the amount of credit claimed, the revenue cost to the federal government, and incentives for taxpayers to increase their spending on energy efficiency improvements—we used the Internal Revenue Service's (IRS) 2009 Statistics of Income (SOI) database, the most current data available, to simulate the effects that different bases would have had on credit claimed, revenue costs, and incentives faced by taxpayers, using actual spending and purchase patterns from the 2009 credit claims. These simulations do not include behavioral responses such as changes in the number of claimants and amounts of spending due to the credit. To conduct these simulations, we examined two alternative bases: a base calculated as a percentage of adjusted gross income (AGI) and a base derived from average spending on different types of improvements. For this objective, we reviewed documentation for the databases we used, conducted electronic checks, and determined that the data presented were sufficiently reliable for our purposes.

Throughout this report, the percentage estimates have a margin of error of plus or minus 5 percentage points, and the estimates of total amounts have a margin of error of plus or minus 5 percent of the estimate.

We conducted this performance audit from August 2010 to April 2012 in accordance with generally accepted government auditing standards. Those standards require that we plan and perform the audit to obtain sufficient, appropriate evidence to provide a reasonable basis for our findings and conclusions based on our audit objectives. We believe that the evidence obtained provides a reasonable basis for our findings based on our audit objectives.

SUMMARY

Under criteria for evaluating a tax credit design, both the performance-based and cost-based credits have advantages and disadvantages with neither design being unambiguously the better option based on current information. Both a cost-based and a performance-based credit are designed to reduce energy use and CO_2 emissions by providing incentives for energy conservation investment. However, they differ in their relative effectiveness and costs. In general, a performance-based credit is more likely to effectively reduce energy use and CO_2 emissions because it rewards energy savings from the investment rather than the cost-based credit's rewarding of spending regardless of whether this spending results in energy savings. However, the performance-based credit may have significant up-front costs for energy audits, not required by the cost-based credit, which could reduce its effectiveness by discouraging investment. In addition, for taxpayers who do invest, these up-front costs may mean that a performance-based credit may have significantly higher taxpayer compliance and IRS administrative costs than a cost-based credit. A credit's fairness depends on subjective judgments of how a credit varies with a taxpayer's income level.

For those taxpayers claiming the 2009 credit, under both base definitions used in our simulations, the total amount of credit claimed fell but taxpayers had a greater incentive to spend more on qualifying products. The incentive was measured as the average effective rate of credit that would apply to additional spending by taxpayers. In 2009, when no base was present, a dollar of additional spending would earn, on average, an additional 10 cents of credit. When the base derived from average spending was introduced in the simulations, a dollar of additional spending earned an estimated 14 to 18 cents of credit. However, because the simulations do not include behavioral responses, the overall effect on revenues and spending of introducing a base is uncertain. For example, introducing a base amount, while likely to limit windfall credits for qualified spending that would have been done anyway, would also make the credit less generous and some taxpayers might no longer use it.

We are not making new recommendations based on this review. This work is intended to assist Congress in considering different ways that the credit can be structured to achieve the stated goals of reducing CO_2 emissions and minimizing U.S. reliance on foreign energy sources.

AGENCY COMMENTS

The Internal Revenue Service, the Department of Energy, and the Department of the Treasury provided us with technical comments after viewing a draft of this report, which we incorporated as appropriate.

J. Christopher
Mihm Managing Director
Strategic Issues

APPENDIX I. BRIEFING SLIDES

Introduction

- Various federal initiatives have sought to address concerns about U.S. reliance on foreign energy sources and the impact of carbon dioxide (CO_2) emissions on the climate.
- One initiative is the nonbusiness energy property credit (I.R.C. §25C),[2] a tax credit that could encourage taxpayers to invest in residential energy efficiency improvements.

Objectives

- To address questions about whether the nonbusiness energy property credit is the best or most effective way to encourage investment in energy efficiency improvements, GAO was asked to:
  - evaluate factors to consider in deciding whether the credit should be cost-based or performance-based, and
  - estimate how requiring that only spending above a minimum amount be eligible for the credit, or introducing a base amount for

    the 2009 credit may have affected measures such as the amount of credit claimed, the revenue cost to the federal government, and incentives for taxpayers to increase their spending on energy efficiency improvements.

- We were also asked for information on use of the credit by spending categories and limits. This information is contained in appendix II.

Summary

- Both the performance-based and cost-based credits have advantages and disadvantages with neither design being unambiguously the better option given current information.
    - The performance-based credit rewards energy savings from the investment rather than, as is the case with the cost-based credit, the spending on investment whether this spending results in energy savings or not.
    - However, the performance-based credit may have significant up-front costs for energy audits, not required by the cost-based credit, which could reduce its effectiveness by discouraging investment and increase its compliance and administrative costs relative to the cost-based credit.
- Under both base definitions used in our simulations, the total amount of credit claimed fell and taxpayers who were already investing in qualifying purchases had a greater incentive to spend more.
    - For example, in 2009, when no base was present, a dollar of additional spending would earn, on average, an additional 10 cents of credit, but when we simulated a base derived from average spending, a dollar of additional spending would earn on average an estimated 14 to 18 cents of credit.
    - However, because the simulations do not include behavioral responses, including the decision to make any initial investment, the overall effect on revenues and spending of introducing a base is uncertain.

Background

2006 and 2007 Credit

- Enacted as part of the Energy Policy Act of 2005,[3] the nonbusiness energy property credit was intended to increase homeowners' investment in energy conserving improvements by reducing their after-tax costs.
  - In 2006 and 2007, the maximum claimable credit was $500.
    - Of this $500, a maximum of $200 could be claimed on exterior windows
    - In all years, any credit amounts exceeding tax liability could not be carried forward.
  - The credit was calculated as 10 percent of qualified spending on insulation systems, exterior windows, exterior doors, and metal roofs.
  - Spending on other types of residential energy property received a 100 percent credit but had credit limits by spending category, specifically:
    - up to $50 for advanced main air circulating fans used in a furnace;
    - up to $150 for furnaces or hot water boilers; and
    - up to $300 for heat pumps, central air conditioning systems, or water heaters.

2009 Credit

- After expiring in 2008, the credit was reauthorized for 2009 and 2010 as part of the American Recovery and Reinvestment Tax Act of 2009
  - the overall credit limit was raised from $500 to $1,500;
  - the rate of credit, which in 2006 and 2007 varied based on the type of spending, was set at 30 percent for all types of qualified spending; and
  - credit limits by spending category were eliminated.
- For 2011, the credit was reauthorized at pre-Recovery Act limits and standards.

Taxpayer Characteristics

Number of claimants, total credit claimed, and total spending in 2006, 2007, and 2009

- In 2006 and 2007, over 4 million taxpayers claimed the credit, and in 2009, the number of claimants increased to almost 7 million.
- From 2006 to 2007, both spending and credit claimed declined, but in 2009, compared to 2007 levels, the total spending more than tripled and the credit claimed increased five-fold.
- The increase in total spending in 2009 may be explained in part by a change in the relevant tax form's instructions, which did not limit the amount the claimant could enter on the form for categories that were previously subject to limits.

Current Design: Elements of Both a Cost- and Performance-Based Credit

- Cost-based credits provide incentives that are usually a fixed percentage of qualified spending, or sometimes, qualified spending above a base amount.

Table 1. Total Returns Filed, Claimants, Spending, and Credit Claimed for the Nonbusiness Energy Property Credit, 2006, 2007, and 2009[4]

Year	Total tax returns filed (mrillions)	Total claimants (millions)	Total spending (millions of dollars)[a]	Total credit claimed (millions of dollars)
2006	138.4	4.3	$7,947	$956
2007	153.6[b]	4.3	$7,484	$938
2009	140.5	6.8	$25,567	$5,288

Source: GAO analysis of IRS data.

[a] Spending reported to IRS in 2006 and 2007 could not exceed certain category limits; for 2009, no category limits were included in the reporting instructions.

[b] For 2007, the aggregate number of returns include those returns that were filed solely to receive an economic stimulus payment. Excluding these returns, 143.0 million returns were filed in 2007.

- Performance-based credits provide incentives that are tied to specific measures of energy savings.
- The nonbusiness energy property credit combines features of both cost-based and performance-based credits.
    - It is cost-based in that the amount of credit claimed is directly proportional to the taxpayer's qualified spending.
    - It is performance-based in that only certain qualifying purchases are eligible.

Design Evaluation: Both Performance- and Cost-Based Credits Are Designed to Conserve Energy and Reduce CO_2 Emissions by Subsidizing Energy Conservation Investment

- The credit's purpose is to reduce inefficient energy consumption and CO_2 emissions.
    - The rationale for providing the tax credit is the view that individuals invest too little from society's point of view when they consider only their own energy cost savings.
    - In addition, there is evidence that taxpayers make too little energy conservation investment based on their own energy costs. They do this, for example, when they underestimate the savings from future operating cost reductions due to their more efficient equipment.
- Both the cost- and performance-based credits address this purpose by providing incentives for energy conservation investment.[5]
    - Who actually benefits from the credit depends on its incidence, i.e., the share of the credit going to producers and consumers of the improvements. If supply is relatively unresponsive to price, a greater share of the benefit would go to producers in the form of higher prices. This result may still be consistent with the purpose of the credit if it promotes the growth of markets for more energy efficient products.
- Ideally, the credit should be designed to reduce individuals' costs sufficiently so that, in the aggregate, their return on investment equals society's return in terms of energy use and CO_2 emission reductions.

Design Evaluation: The Performance-Based Credit Better Targets Conservation Investment But Its Higher Initial Costs May Discourage Some Investment

- For a better chance of producing the intended benefit, the credit should target activities that most directly promote the credit's purpose and provide sufficient incentives for taxpayers to increase these activities.
- The performance-based credit is likely to better target conservation investment spending.
    - The performance-based credit provides fixed amounts of credit for achieving different levels of energy savings. It therefore provides an incentive for taxpayers to minimize the spending required to achieve a given amount of energy savings. The credit is designed to reward additional energy savings and CO_2 reductions but not additional spending.
    - The cost-based credit is designed to reward spending on conservation investment that may, or may not, lead ultimately to additional energy savings.
- However, the relative effectiveness of the incentives provided by performance-based and cost-based credits is less certain.
    - Performance based credits are likely to have larger up-front costs than cost-based credits and may discourage taxpayers from buying qualifying energy savings products.
        - These costs include energy audits to establish a baseline of energy use against which to measure improvements and possibly post-improvement audits to confirm that energy savings have been realized. These added costs could reduce the incentive to undertake any investments.
        - On the other hand, such audits might also increase participation if they reassure taxpayers that they will actually save energy.

Design Evaluation: Performance-Based Credits May Have Significantly Higher Compliance And Administrative Costs Than Cost-Based Credits

- To assess the credit design, the benefits likely to be produced by the credit should be compared to its costs, which include the lost tax revenue and IRS administrative costs as well as more indirect costs, such as taxpayer compliance burden and economic efficiency costs.

- Performance-based credits may have significantly higher compliance and administrative costs than cost-based credits.
  - Taxpayer compliance costs are higher due to up-front costs, such as energy audits not required by cost-based credits.
  - According to IRS officials, administration costs are likely to be higher for performance- based credits that reward measurable (not estimated) increases in energy efficiency because examinations would have to verify that improvements were made, not just that money was spent.
- The relative economic efficiency costs of the alternative credit designs are uncertain because their effects depend on the degree to which the credits alter decisions to spend across different improvement types and how much they reduce energy use and CO_2 emissions. The effects are difficult to infer from design alone.
- The relative effect of a cost-based credit and performance-based credit on revenue costs is uncertain because it depends chiefly on whether the credit has base amounts and limits and which credit rates are chosen.

Design Evaluation: The Fairness of How The Credit's Costs and Benefits Are Distributed Depends on Subjective Value Judgments

- The fairness of the credit's design depends on the judgment of whoever is evaluating the design.
  - Views on what is a fair distribution of the credit's costs and benefits can differ dramatically across individuals.
- However, whatever one's views of fairness, an analysis of the distribution of costs and benefits by such factors as income level can be useful.
- Under an ability to pay principle of fairness, fairness requires that those who are more capable of bearing the burden of a tax should pay more. Equivalently, for a tax credit, they should receive less of the benefit.
  - Those who adopt an ability-to-pay principle of fairness may view as unfair a distribution where lower income taxpayers receive lower benefits from the credit than higher income taxpayers.
- However, under the same principle, fairness requires that taxpayers who have the same ability to pay should bear the same tax burden, or in this case, receive the same benefit.

- Those who adopt this principle may view as unfair that taxpayers who invest in energy conservation have lower tax liabilities than taxpayers with the same income who do not invest.

Introducing a Base

Credit Design Features

- As currently designed, all qualified spending up to the various limits is eligible for the nonbusiness energy property credit. This design increases the likelihood of windfall credits being earned for spending on qualifying energy efficient investments that would have occurred without the credit.
- A base that would eliminate windfall benefits would reward only the additional spending that taxpayers make due to the availability of the credit.
  - The credit amount would be calculated as the credit rate multiplied by the amount of qualified spending in excess of the base amount.
  - A base that eliminates windfalls is difficult to determine because it requires estimating how much consumers would spend on the types of products qualifying for the credit if the credit did not exist.
  - Because such a base amount is difficult to determine, other tax credits, such as the research tax credit, use proxies for these unknown amounts.

Effects on the Use of the Credit

- Introducing a base can affect use of the credit in two opposite ways:
  - The base can reduce the take-up rate of the credit, i.e., the number of taxpayers making qualifying purchases.
    - Because the amount of credit on spending only over a base amount generally would be less than a credit on the full amount of spending on a qualifying purchase, some taxpayers may choose to make no investment at all.
    - Several factors could affect the taxpayers' decision to invest, such as the amount of spending that is "reactive," reflecting investment that cannot be postponed because of, for example, equipment failure.

- The base can increase the amount of spending on qualifying purchases by those who choose to invest.
  - For those who have made the decision to invest, i.e., who are "in the market," the base can increase the incentive for additional spending.
    - In particular, claimants constrained by credit limits (about 25 percent of claimants in 2009) may find that more of any additional spending will be eligible for the credit.
- The simulations in this report focus on this second effect and do not include the effects on spending due to any change in the number of taxpayers choosing to make an investment.

Determining the Base

- Bases or floors that are currently part of the Internal Revenue Code include amounts calculated as a percentage of income (such as the floor on deductions for medical expenses) or spending (such as the research tax credit).
- Following this precedent in the code, the base for the nonbusiness energy property credit could be calculated as a percentage of each taxpayer's qualified spending or adjusted gross income (AGI).
  - This option could reduce the administrative costs of the base because it uses only the information reported on tax returns.[6]
- The base could also be calculated using price information on nonqualifying improvements.
  - The rationale is that such prices may be used to better approximate the spending that the taxpayer would have done without the credit.
  - Department of Energy (DOE) currently collects information on the costs of many types of energy efficient home improvements.
  - However, DOE indicates that because prices vary so widely across locations, it would be very difficult to construct a base from these prices that would apply nationally.
  - Setting bases that vary by location and product type would increase the administrative costs of the credit.

The Base Used in the Simulations

- To illustrate the effects of introducing a base amount, we recalculated the amount of credit taxpayers would have claimed and estimated how incentives to use the credit would have changed under alternative base definitions, for the pattern of spending observed in 2009.

- Percentage of AGI base: We calculated the AGI base as a percentage of the taxpayers' adjusted gross income where, for each category, this percentage was the average amount spent by claimants in 2009 as a share of their AGI.
- Average spending base: We calculated the average spending base as the average of actual 2009 spending in each improvement category.

- It is not known how the credit take-up rate or spending would change if a base were introduced. We adjusted the base amount by a range of values--which we call the base rates--to show how sensitive our estimates of incentives and credit claimed are to the size of the base. The simulations used 25 percent, 50 percent, and 75 percent of these category bases as base rates.
    - When implementing a base, policymakers may wish to consider trade-offs between take-up rates and incentives for induced spending. All else equal, a lower base may have a less discouraging effect on the decision to invest but is more likely to reward spending that would have been done anyway.
- The simulations were run using the 2009 IRS Statistics of Income (SOI) database of individual tax returns and show what credit would have been claimed and other results if the different bases had been in effect. The comparison of the results of the simulations to the actual 2009 data shows the effects of introducing the bases.

Illustration of How to Calculate Credits Using the Average Spending Base

- The graph on the next slide illustrates the calculation of the base amount for the average spending base.
    - The spending type in this example is windows and the amount of qualified spending is $4,000.
    - Average qualified spending for windows by all taxpayers in 2009 was $3,665.
    - The base amount was calculated using the lowest base rate as 25 percent of average spending which is equal to $916.
        - If this base were implemented, IRS would, based on the most recent tax return data available, provide taxpayers the base

amount--taxpayers would not be expected to calculate this amount.

- The credit is calculated as the difference between the qualified spending of $4,000 and the base amount of $916, which is equal to $3,084, multiplied by the credit rate of 30 percent, or about $925 of credit.

Illustrative Example of a Taxpayer Spending $4,000 on Windows (Average Spending Base)

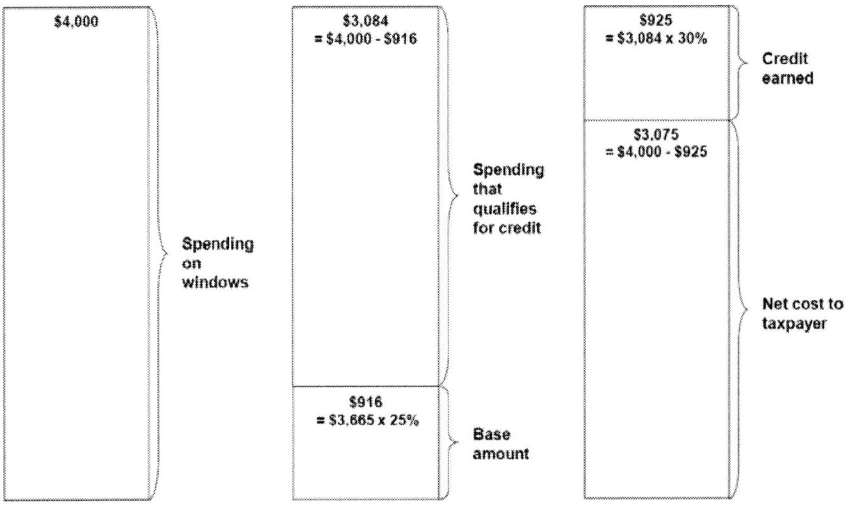

Average spending base (average spending = $3,665; base rate = 25%)

Illustration of How to Calculate Credits Using the Percentage of AGI Base

- The graph on the next slide illustrates the calculation of the base amount for the percentage of AGI base.
    - As in the previous example, the spending type is windows and the amount of qualified spending is $4,000.
    - AGI for this taxpayer is $25,000 and qualified spending on windows as an average share of income was about 5.1 percent in 2009.
    - The base amount for this taxpayer, using the lowest base rate of 25 percent, is equal to 1.275 percent of $25,000 of AGI (25

percent of the 5.1 percent share of income) which is equal to about $319.

- If this base were implemented, taxpayers would be given the percentages corresponding to their level of AGI with their tax returns.

- The credit is the difference between the qualified spending of $4,000 and the base amount of $319, which is equal to $3,681, multiplied by the credit rate of 30 percent, or about $1,104 of credit.

Illustrative Example of a Taxpayer Spending $4,000 on Windows (AGI Base)

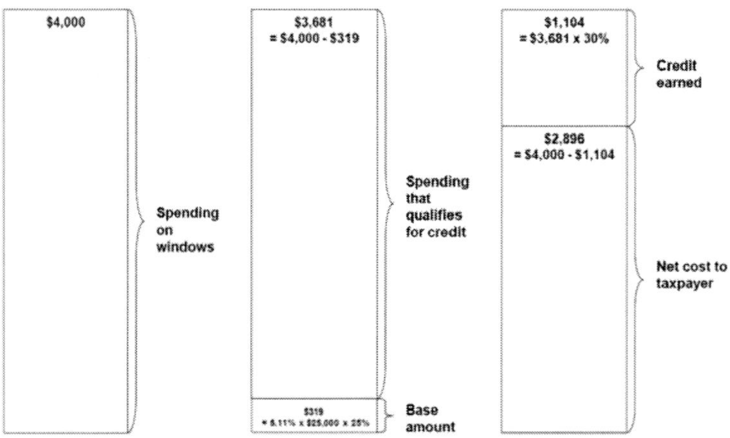

AGI base (average share of AGI spent = 5.11%; AGI = $25,000; base rate = 25%)

Illustration of Base Amounts, Qualified Spending, and Credit Amounts under Different Base Definitions and Base Rates

- The table on the next slide shows base spending and credit amounts for the average spending base under different assumptions about the base rates.
- The table also shows base, spending and credit amounts for the percentage of AGI base under different assumptions about the base rates and AGI.
- The total credit amount declines for both base types as the base rate increases.
- The credit amount for the percentage of income base decreases as income increases.

- With the AGI base, a lower-income taxpayer will earn more credit than a higher income taxpayer spending the same amount. In the examples, the AGI base equals 5.11% of income multiplied by a base rate. For any base rate, the base amount increases as income rises so lower income taxpayers have a lower base. In the examples, taxpayers are assumed to spend $4,000 on windows, regardless of income, and the amount of spending that qualifies for credit is larger for lower-income taxpayers with a lower base.

Illustrative Example of a Taxpayer Spending $4,000 on Windows

Average spending base (average spending on windows in 2009 = $3,665)									
	Base amount (by base rate)			**Spending qualifying for the credit (by base rate)**			**Credit earned (by base rate)**		
	25%	50%	75%	25%	50%	75%	25%	50%	75%
	$ 916	$ 1,833	$ 2,749	$ 3,084	$ 2,168	$ 1,251	$925	$650	$375
Adjusted gross income base (average share of AGI spent on windows = 5.11 percent)									
AGI	**Base amount (by base rate)**			**Spending qualifying for the credit (by base rate)**			**Credit earned (by base rate)**		
	25%	**50%**	**75%**	**25%**	**50%**	**75%**	**25%**	**50%**	**75%**
$25,000	$ 319	$ 639	$ 958	$ 3,681	$ 3,361	$ 3,042	$ 1,104	$ 1,008	$913
$75,000	$ 958	$ 1,916	$ 2,874	$ 3,042	$ 2,084	$ 1,126	$913	$625	$338
$150,000	$ 1,916	$ 3,833	$ 5,749	$ 2,084	$ 167	$0	$625	$50	$0

Source: GAO analysis of IRS data.

Simulated Effects on Credit Claimed and Marginal Incentives in 2009 of Alternative Base Definitions

- In 2009, about $5.3 billion was claimed in nonbusiness energy property credit, and across all claimants the average marginal incentive was about 10 percent.
    - The average marginal incentive is the percentage change in the amount of credit associated with an increase or decrease in spending, divided by the percentage change in spending, averaged across all claimants.

Simulated Effects on Credit Claimed and Marginal Incentives of Alternative Base Definitions in 2009

Base definition	2009 credit	Simulated credit with average spending base			Simulated credit with AGI base		
		Low–25 percent	Medium –50 percent	High–75 percent	Low–25 percent	Medium –50 percent	High–75 percent
Total credit earned (billions of dollars)	**5.3**	4.2	3.3	2.6	3.9	2.9	2.1
Average marginal incentive	**10%**	14%	16%	18%	15%	18%	21%

Source: GAO analysis of IRS data.

    - In this case, on average, a dollar of additional spending would earn an additional 10 cents of credit, or equivalently, would reduce the cost of a dollar of additional spending by 10 cents.
- In simulations introducing a base spending amount, the amount of credit claimed fell, and the average marginal incentive to use the credit rose.
    - Introducing a base amount reduced the revenue cost of the credit to the government and simultaneously gave taxpayers a stronger incentive to invest in qualifying energy efficiency improvements.
    - Because the simulations do not include behavioral responses, the actual effect of introducing a base on revenues and spending is uncertain. Taxpayers facing a stronger incentive to use the credit may spend more than they otherwise would, increasing both the revenue cost of the credit and the amount spent on energy efficiency improvements. However, a base would also make the credit less generous overall, which could reduce the number of claimants, decreasing both the revenue cost of the credit and the amount spent on energy efficiency improvements.
    - Taxpayers with more than $100,000 in AGI generally accounted for a smaller share of credit claimed in simulations with an AGI base. For example, taxpayers with AGI between $250,000 and $500,000 claimed about 4.1 percent of credit in 2009 and between 1.5 and 2.9 percent of total credit in these simulations.
    - Under the AGI base, taxpayers with AGI between $80,000 and $100,000 accounted for about the same share of credit claimed as the share of credit they actually claimed in 2009.
- Simulating a base amount derived from average spending on qualifying purchases produced an opposite but less pronounced effect on the share of credit claimed by these income groups.
    - Taxpayers with AGI between $0 and $80,000 claimed a smaller share of credit than they actually claimed in 2009. For example, in simulations with an average spending base, taxpayers with between $20,000 and $40,000 in AGI claimed anywhere from about 8.1 percent to 9.4 percent of total credit, depending on the base rate, always less than the 10.2 percent of credit they claimed in 2009.

Distributional Effects of the Alternative Bases

Adjusted gross income (dollars in thousands	Percentage of all taxpayers with AGI > 0 in 2009	Share of credit claimed						
		2009	Simulated credit with an AGI base			Simulated credit with an average spending base		
			High	Medium	Low	High	Medium	Low
$0-$20	33.7%	0.8%	1.5%	1.2%	1.0%	0.6%	0.6%	0.7%
$20-$40	24.0	10.2	16.3	14.0	12.0	8.1	8.7	9.4
$40-$60	14.1	16.8	22.0	20.2	18.5	14.0	15.0	15.9
$60-$80	9.3	18.4	20.5	20.2	19.5	17.1	17.7	18.1
$80-$100	6.3	15.4	14.8	15.3	15.5	15.2	15.3	15.4
$100-$125	4.7	12.8	10.8	11.6	12.3	13.6	13.3	13.0
$125-$150	2.6	7.9	5.5	6.5	7.2	8.7	8.4	8.1
$150-$250	3.6	12.2	7.2	8.7	10.6	15.0	13.9	13.1
$250-$500	1.3	4.1	1.5	1.9	2.9	5.6	5.0	4.6
Greater than$500	0.5	1.5	0.2	0.3	0.5	2.2	1.9	1.7

Source: GAO analysis of IRS data.

- Taxpayers with AGI over $100,000 claimed a larger share of credit in simulations with an average spending base than they actually claimed in 2009. For example, taxpayers with AGI between $250,000 and $500,000 claimed between 4.6 and 5.6 of total credit in these simulations, as compared to 4.1 percent of total credit in 2009.

Conclusion

- The nonbusiness energy property credit has been claimed by millions of taxpayers since it was first introduced in 2006.
- While making the credit performance based likely would result in greater reductions in energy use than does the current credit, the performance based design is not clearly superior given current information because the performance-based credit likely would have greater taxpayer and government compliance and administration costs.
- If the cost-based credit is retained and a base spending amount was required, taxpayers who make qualifying purchases would have a greater incentive to spend more on such purchases and windfall benefits to those who would have made purchases without the credit would be reduced. However, a base spending requirement would reduce the absolute amount of credit taxpayers receive for qualifying purchases and might therefore result in fewer taxpayers making such purchases.
- Further, a base that excludes only windfall spending is difficult to construct. Proxy bases may over- or under correct for windfall benefits. A comprehensive evaluation of proxies for windfall spending would assess their effect on windfalls and their net effect on additional spending on qualified energy saving purchases.

APPENDIX II. USE OF THE NONBUSINESS ENERGY PROPERTY CREDIT BY SPENDING CATEGORIES AND LIMITS

- About 5 million out of 6.8 million total claimants, or about 73 percent of all claimants, reported spending on only one type of energy improvement in 2009. Their qualified spending of about $16.7 billion accounts for about 65 percent of spending by all claimants.

- About 1.1 million of these claimants, or about 23 percent, were subject to the overall credit limit of $1,500, with close to 400,000 of these returns reporting spending on windows. About 6% of claimants reporting spending on only one type of improvement had limited tax liability that constrained the amount of credit claimed.
- A similar analysis of how spending was affected by limits for claimants reporting spending on more than one kind of improvement would be difficult. For instance, it is not possible to attribute their limited use of the credit to a particular category of spending, since constraints related to the overall credit limit or tax liability depend on total spending in all categories.
- The next three slides show the number of claimants and amount of spending by spending categories according to whether taxpayers were:
    - unconstrained by any of the credit's limits
    - constrained by the overall limit
    - constrained by the tax liability limit

Table 1. Use of the Nonbusiness Energy Property Credit by Unconstrained Claimants in 2009

Retrofit type	Claimants reporting spending on only one type of retrofit		Claimants reporting spending on more than one type of retrofit	
	Number	Spending (in millions)	Number	Spending (in millions)
Insulation	848,490	$947.0	644,100	$453.9
Windows	765,600	$1,605.2	619,284	$726.4
Doors	754,523	$811.3	681,297	$522.3
Roofs	107,659	$291.5	95,388	$136.2
Energy efficient building property	387,210	$875.1	132,373	$166.8
Furnaces and hot water boilers	608,467	$1251.0	214,217	$256.1
Furnace fans	52,218	$115.3	59,543	$57.2
All retrofit types	3,524,166	$5,896.3	1,060,682	$2,318.9

Source: GAO analysis of IRS data.

These tax returns account for about 68 percent of all claimants and about 32 percent of total spending in 2009. Because their use of the nonbusiness energy property credit is unconstrained, their credit claimed equals 30 percent of their spending, which is about 47 percent of all credit claimed.

Table 2. Use of the Nonbusiness Energy Property Credit by Claimants Subject to the Overall Credit Limit of $1,500 in 2009

Retrofit type	Claimants reporting spending on only one type of retrofit		Claimants reporting spending on more than one type of retrofit	
	Number	Spending (in millions)	Number	Spending (in millions)
Insulation	107,303	$850.8	281,604	$794.5
Windows	393,447	$3,635.8	425,030	$2,060.9
Doors	21,546	$160.2	319,995	$630.0
Roofs	86,786	$792.1	114,725	$676.5
Energy efficient building property	245,143	$1,944.9	139,584	$688.7
Furnaces and hot water boilers	237,430	$1,810.5	161,846	$735.7
Furnace fans	33,193	$252.0	54,008	$178.4
All retrofit types	**1,124,848**	**$9,446.3**	**594,234**	**$5,764.8**

Source: GAO analysis of IRS data.

These tax returns account for about 25 percent of all claimants and about 59 percent of total spending in 2009. Because of the overall credit limit, their credit claimed is less than 30 percent of their spending and is around 49 percent of all credit claimed.

Table 3. Use of the Nonbusiness Energy Property Credit by Claimants with Limited Tax Liability in 2009

Retrofit type	Claimants reporting spending on only one type of retrofit		Claimants reporting spending on more than one type of retrofit	
	Number	Spending (in millions)	Number	Spending (in millions)
Insulation	37,837	$118.5	70,361	$118.1
Windows	77,150	$405.5	90,071	$254.5
Doors	29,645	$52.7	82,309	$94.9
Roofs	28,871	$166.9	34,955	$120.0
Energy efficient building property	52,861	$276.0	34,693	$95.4

Table 3. (Continued)

Retrofit type	Claimants reporting spending on only one type of retrofit		Claimants reporting spending on more than one type of retrofit	
	Number	Spending (in millions)	Number	Spending (in millions)
Furnaces and hot water boilers	66,366	$296.8	30,112	$54.6
Furnace fans	11,592	$56.9	14,434	$30.0
All retrofit types	**304,322**	**$1,373.3**	**142,698**	**$767.7**

Source: GAO analysis of IRS data.

These tax returns account for about 7 percent of all claimants and about 8 percent of total spending in 2009. Because of limited tax liability, their credit claimed is less than 30 percent of their spending and equals about 5 percent of all credit claimed.

End Notes

[1] I.R.C. § 25C.

[2] Energy Policy Act of 2005, Pub. L. No. 109-58, § 1333, 119 Stat. 594 (Aug. 8, 2005).

[3] Pub. L. No. 109-58, § 1333, 119 Stat. 594 (Aug. 8, 2005).

[4] GAO estimates were computed using the SOI advance 2009 Individual Complete Report. In our computations, the nonbusiness energy property credit is applied against tax liability remaining after all other credits are taken into account.

[5] While both credit designs address the purpose of the credit, they do so indirectly by promoting conservation investment. Another, more direct method of reducing energy use and CO_2 emissions that has been suggested is a carbon tax on energy consumption.

[6] the actual spending on qualifying investments would need to be calculated by IRS from information on prior tax year returns.

In: Residential Energy Tax Credits
Editor: Lena Kingston
ISBN: 978-1-63321-717-1

Chapter 3

PROCESSES WERE NOT ESTABLISHED TO VERIFY ELIGIBILITY FOR RESIDENTIAL ENERGY CREDITS*

Treasury Inspector General for Tax Administration

ABBREVIATIONS

e-filed, e-file	Electronically filed; electronic file
IRS	Internal Revenue Service
TIGTA	Treasury Inspector General for Tax Administration

BACKGROUND

The American Recovery and Reinvestment Act of 2009 (Recovery Act)[1] made important changes to the law relating to energy credits. The Recovery Act modified the provisions for both the Nonbusiness Energy Property Credit and the Residential Energy Efficient Property Credit. The modifications to the Nonbusiness Energy Property Credit were to encourage the purchase of energy efficient property for an individual's principal residence that were designed to reduce heat loss during cold months or heat gain during warm months. The

* This is an edited, reformatted and augmented version of report number 2011-41-038, issued April 19, 2011.

Residential Energy Efficient Property Credit is for use in an individual's principal or secondary residence to encourage the purchase of renewable sources of energy for use in a home. The amount of both of the Residential Energy Credits allowed reduces an individual's taxes owed.

- ***Nonbusiness Energy Property Credit*** – allows individuals to take a credit of 30 percent of the costs paid or incurred in Calendar Year 2009 for energy efficient products for their principal residence with a maximum of $1,500 total for Tax Years 2009 and 2010. Energy efficient products, such as windows and doors, had to be placed in an individual's existing principal residence. New construction and rental property not owned and occupied by the individual when the energy saving improvements were made do not qualify for this Credit.
- ***Residential Energy Efficient Property Credit*** – allows individuals to take a credit for investments in alternative energy equipment[2] for their principal residence or secondary residence. This Credit generally equals 30 percent of qualifying alternative energy equipment costs with no dollar limit. Alternative energy equipment, like a geothermal heat pump or wind energy system, could be placed in an individual's newly constructed or existing principal or secondary residence. However, individuals claiming this Credit for a fuel cell system[3] have to install it in their principal residence to qualify for this Credit. Rental property does not qualify for the Credit.

For both of the above energy credits, the individual's principal (or secondary, if applicable) residence must be located in the United States. The individual's principal (or secondary, if applicable) residence can include a house, manufactured home, mobile home, condominium, cooperative apartment, or houseboat. Both credits are claimed on the Residential Energy Credits (Form 5695)[4] that is included with an individual's U.S. Individual Income Tax Return (Form 1040). Figure 1 identifies the volumes of tax returns and Residential Energy Credits allowed for Tax Year 2009.

Type of Tax Return Filed	Volume	Energy Credits Allowed
Paper	1,601,687	$1,512,642,024
Electronic	5,183,701	$4,313,474,451
Totals	**6,785,388**	**$5,826,116,475**

Source: Tax return data for Processing Year 2010 as of Cycle 52 (December 31, 2010).

Figure 1. Tax Year 2009 Tax Returns With Claimed Residential Energy Credits Allowed.

The 2010 Filing Season Review Identified Some Problems with the Processing of Residential Energy Credits

The Treasury Inspector General for Tax Administration (TIGTA) 2010 Filing Season report[5] determined that:

- ***Individuals were allowed energy credits exceeding the maximum amounts.*** Our review identified 171 individuals claiming $453,220 in erroneous Nonbusiness Energy Property Credits for Tax Year 2009. These individuals claimed a credit that exceeded the maximum allowable amount of $1,500 for all filing filing statuses reporting only one principal residence (or $3,000 for married filing jointly in certain circumcumstances).[6] The audit determined that programming of an *electronic file (e-file)* reject code had not been implemented to prevent individuals from claiming a Nonbusiness Energy Property Credit exceeding the maximum allowable amount. Internal Revenue Service (IRS) management agreed to ensure computer systems are programmed to identify individuals exceeding the maximum allowable Nonbusiness Energy Property Credit. This included programming to reject *e-filed* tax returns with this condition.
- ***The IRS was unable to accurately track and account for both types of energy credits claimed on*** *****5**********. Our review identified that the IRS cannot accurately track and account for both types of energy credits claimed ***5**********. ******5***********5***************, the amounts of Residential Energy Credits are included on a line on the Form 1040 with two additional tax credits. The IRS has programming in place to identify tax returns with any amount claimed on this line. Tax examiners then review the tax returns and move the amounts into appropriate fields. The Form 5695 has two credits, the Nonbusiness Energy Property Credit and the Residential Energy Efficient Property Credit. The IRS combines the amounts for these two credits into one field, Residential Energy Credits. Combining the two credits into one total ***5********* impairs the IRS's ability to accurately report the number of claims and the respective amounts paid for the Nonbusiness Energy Property Credit and the Residential Energy Efficient Property Credit.

Recovery Act activities require a high level of scrutiny, and taxpayer dollars spent on economic recovery must be subject to unprecedented levels of transparency and accountability. Federal agencies are required to ensure Recovery Act funds are used for authorized purposes and appropriate measures are taken to prevent fraud, waste, and abuse. As such, the TIGTA is required to monitor the IRS's implementation of Recovery Act provisions, and this audit was conducted to meet those requirements.

This review was performed at the Wage and Investment Division Headquarters in Atlanta, Georgia, and the Submission Processing Site in Kansas City, Missouri, during the period September 2010 through February 2011. We conducted this performance audit in accordance with generally accepted government auditing standards. Those standards require that we plan and perform the audit to obtain sufficient, appropriate evidence to provide a reasonable basis for our findings and conclusions based on our audit objective. We believe that the evidence obtained provides a reasonable basis for our findings and conclusions based on our audit objective. Detailed information on our audit objective, scope, and methodology is presented in Appendix I. Major contributors to the report are listed in Appendix II.

RESULTS OF REVIEW

The Internal Revenue Service Cannot Verify Eligibility for Residential Energy Credits at the Time a Tax Return Is Processed

The IRS cannot verify whether individuals claiming Residential Energy Credits are entitled to them at the time their tax returns are processed. The IRS does not require individuals to provide any third-party documentation supporting the purchase of qualifying home improvement products and/or costs associated with making energy efficiency improvements and if these qualified purchases and/or improvements were made to their residence. Instead, the IRS relies on individuals claiming the Residential Energy Credits to comply with tax laws and to provide correct information on their tax returns. Figure 2 shows the key requirements for claiming Residential Energy Credits that the IRS cannot verify at the time a tax return is processed.

Key Requirement	Can the IRS Verify When the Tax Return Is Processed?
Individual Purchased a Qualified Energy Saving Product and/or Made Energy Efficiency Improvements	No
Cost of Energy Saving Improvements	No
Energy Saving Improvements Made to the Individual's Home	No
Time Period Costs/Improvements Made	No

Source: IRS procedures and tax form instructions.

Figure 2. Key Residential Energy Credit Requirements the IRS Is Unable to Verify.

Individuals with No Record of Owning Residential Property Claimed Erroneous Residential Energy Credits

We reviewed a statistically valid sample of 150 tax returns from individuals who were allowed Residential Energy Credits. We did not project a noncompliance rate to the population using this sample because of the potential for omissions or errors in this type of third-party reporting.

Our computer analysis of 6,466,981 Tax Year 2009 tax returns with Residential Energy Credits processed between January 1, 2010, and July 23, 2010, identified 302,063 (5 percent) that did not show any indication of home ownership. Residential Energy Credits claimed on these tax returns totaled more than $234 million.

Our research of third-party data for a statistically valid sample of 150 of these 302,063 tax returns identified:

- 105 (70 percent) for which the individuals owned a home.
- 45 (30 percent) for which the individuals had no record of owning a home. These individuals claimed $30,201 in potentially erroneous Residential Energy Credits, resulting in a net tax effect of $29,962. To determine if the individuals claiming these credits owned a principal residence, we used the same third-party vendor information that the IRS uses when examining questionable tax returns. The third-party vendor receives property deed data from all of the 50 States, and the District of Columbia and the Virgin Islands. Most States send

property deed data monthly to this third-party vendor, with some States providing the data more frequently.

The Office of Management and Budget has established five broad requirements that all agencies must follow in order to meet accountability objectives relating to Recovery Act funds. These requirements are posted on Recovery.gov. The third requirement is that Federal agencies ensure Recovery Act funds are used for authorized purposes and take steps needed to mitigate instances of fraud, waste, and abuse. The IRS has not established processes to ensure individuals are appropriately claiming Residential Energy Credits. In addition to the IRS not requesting any third-party information to verify Residential Energy Credits claimed, the Form 5695 does not require individuals to provide the information, which could serve as a deterrent for those individuals who intend to erroneously claim these credits.

IRS management noted that they had no plans during Filing Season 2010 to select and perform post-processing reviews focusing on individuals that claim Residential Energy Credits. However, in its Compliance 2011 Plan, the IRS states that it will review ****5******************5*********** *******.

Recommendation

Recommendation 1

The Commissioner, Wage and Investment Division, should revise the Form 5695 to request specific information supporting key eligibility requirements that could be used to verify requirements were met and may serve as a deterrent for those individuals who intend to erroneously claim these credits. For example, the Form 5695 revisions could include requiring the address of the residence for which the qualified energy-saving product and/or energy efficiency improvement was made, whether the product and/or improvement was made to their principal or secondary residence, and whether the residence was new construction or an existing structure.

Management's Response

IRS management agreed with this recommendation. Form 5695, Residential Energy Credits, will be revised to request specific information concerning the property, such as requiring the specific address, whether the property was the primary or secondary residence, and whether the improvements were made as part of building a new home or modifying an existing home.

Erroneous Residential Energy Credits Were Allowed to Ineligible Individuals Even Though the Internal Revenue Service Had Data to Identify These Claims during Tax Return Processing

We identified 362 ineligible individuals who were allowed to erroneously claim $404,578 in Residential Energy Credits on their tax returns. This occurred because the IRS did not develop a process to identify prisoners or individuals who were under the age needed to enter into a contract to purchase a residence claiming the credits. Moreover, the IRS has data that could have been used to identify these erroneous credits.

Figure 3 below shows the breakdown of the ineligible individuals who were allowed the Residential Energy Credits.

Prisoners Were Erroneously Allowed $343,487 in Residential Energy Credits in Tax Year 2009 Even Though They Were in Prison for the Entire Year

We determined that 262 prisoners who filed tax returns as single or head of household were allowed Residential Energy Credits totaling $343,487, although they were in prison for all of Tax Year 2009 when these energy-saving improvements were purportedly purchased. The IRS has data that can be used to identify prisoners erroneously claiming these credits.

Type of Ineligible Claimant	Number of Individuals	Amount Allowed
Prisoner	262	$343,487
Underage	100	$61,091
Total	**362**	**$404,578**

Source: TIGTA analysis of IRS computer files.

Figure 3. Breakdown of Ineligible Individuals[7]

Underage Individuals Were Erroneously Allowed $61,091 in Residential Energy Credits

We identified 100 individuals under the age of 18 (26 of these were under the age of 14) who were allowed $61,091 in Residential Energy Credits. The youngest individual receiving the credit was 3 years old. Contract law generally exempts children under the age of 18 from being bound by the terms of a contract. Therefore, it is unlikely that these individuals would have entered into an arms-length transaction for the purchase of a residence. The IRS has data that can be used to identify underage individuals erroneously claiming these credits.

Recommendations

The Commissioner, Wage and Investment Division, should:

Recommendation 2

Examine the tax returns of the 362 individuals we identified as being in prison or underage to determine whether these individuals qualify for the Residential Energy Credits.

Management's Response

IRS management partially agreed with this recommendation. The IRS will review the returns of the 362 individuals identified as being in prison or underage and will audit those returns that warrant further examination.

Recommendation 3

Ensure processes are implemented to identify and review tax returns filed by prisoners or underage individuals to ensure they qualify for Residential Energy Credits claimed.

Management's Response

IRS management agreed with this recommendation. The IRS has processes in place to identify returns filed by prisoners, underage individuals, and others that are questionable and appear to improperly claim credits and deductions. Although these processes were developed to provide more stringent screening for higher risk returns claiming refundable credits, such as the Earned Income Tax Credit, the First-Time Homebuyer Credit, and the Adoption Credit, that screening process is not restricted to those high-risk items. The Residential Energy Credits, along with other items of income, deductions, and credits, are also subject to review and contribute to the factors evaluated in selecting returns for examination.

The IRS continuously assesses and evaluates compliance risks in meeting the goal of a balanced compliance program that strategically addresses the most egregious noncompliance across all taxpayer segments. As part of the IRS's ongoing research efforts and its 2011 American Recovery and Reinvestment Act Examination plan, it will review a sample of Residential Energy Credit cases in a post-refund environment. Those warranting examination will be selected for audit, and the results will be factored into future American Recovery and Reinvestment Act examination plans.

APPENDIX I. DETAILED OBJECTIVE, SCOPE, AND METHODOLOGY

The overall objective of this review was to assess the effectiveness of the IRS's process to identify erroneous Residential Energy Credits. To accomplish this objective, we:

I. Determined the actions taken by the IRS to identify erroneous Residential Energy Credit claims.
   A. Participated in a walkthrough at the IRS Submission Processing Site in Kansas City, Missouri, to determine efforts taken by IRS functions to identify erroneous Residential Energy Credit claims.
   B. Interviewed IRS management and analysts in the Code and Edit, Error Resolution, and Examination functions to identify steps taken to verify the accuracy of Residential Energy Credit claims.
   C. Reviewed Internal Revenue Code Section 25C (Nonbusiness Energy Property Credit), Internal Revenue Code Section 25D (Residential Energy Efficient Property Credit), and Internal Revenue Manual sections pertaining to the processing of individual income tax returns with Residential Energy Credits, as well as IRS tax forms and publications used to process individual tax returns with Residential Energy Credits.

II. Determined whether individuals are accurately claiming Residential Energy Credits on their tax returns.
   A. Selected a statistically valid sample of 150 tax returns of 302,063 Tax Year 2009 individual tax returns with allowed Residential Energy Credits and no indicators of home ownership and rental property ownership to assess the actions taken by the IRS to validate these tax credits.[8] The returns were processed on the

IRS's Individual Master File/Individual Return Transaction File[9] between January 1, 2010, and
July 23, 2010. We used attribute sampling to calculate the minimum sample size n, which was rounded to 150:

$n = (Z^2 p (1-p))/ (A^2)$

Z = Confidence Level:	90 percent (expressed as 1.65 standard deviation)
p = Expected Rate of Occurrence:	5 percent
A = Precision Rate:	±3 percent

1. Used the third-party property research tool to identify property records to determine whether allowed Residential Energy Credits met the legal requirements of Internal Revenue Code Sections 25C and 25D.

III. Determined whether the IRS allowed ineligible individuals to claim Residential Energy Credits.

A. Matched 6,466,981 Tax Year 2009 individual income tax returns with Residential Energy Credits to the IRS's 2009 Prisoner File[10] to identify prisoners. We validated the accuracy of the data from the match by comparing a judgmental sample of 25 of the individuals identified as prisoners to the information residing on the IRS's Integrated Data Retrieval System.

1. Matched only Prisoner File individuals with a filing status of single or head of household.
2. Matched only Prisoner File individuals in prison for all of Tax Year 2009.

B. Matched 6,466,981 Tax Year 2009 individual income tax returns with Residential Energy Credits to the IRS's National Account Profile[11] to identify individuals under age 18. The computer file of tax return data was assessed for reliability by the TIGTA Office of Information Services. The National Account Profile data were assessed for reliability by the TIGTA Data Center Warehouse. We validated the accuracy of the data by reviewing a judgmental sample of 25 individuals whose age is less than 18 and comparing the data to the information residing on the IRS's Integrated Data Retrieval System.

Internal Controls Methodology

Internal controls relate to management's plans, methods, and procedures used to meet their mission, goals, and objectives. Internal controls include the processes and procedures for planning, organizing, directing, and controlling program operations. They include the systems for measuring, reporting, and monitoring program performance. We determined the following internal controls were relevant to our audit objective: the American Recovery and Reinvestment Act of 2009;[12] the Internal Revenue Manual; the *Standards for Internal Control in the Federal Government;*[13] and the IRS's policies, procedures, and practices for processing Residential Energy Credits. We evaluated these controls by interviewing IRS tax processing personnel, examining applicable information, and reviewing samples of tax returns with Residential Energy Credits.

APPENDIX II, MAJOR CONTRIBUTORS TO THIS REPORT

Michael E. McKenney, Assistant Inspector General for Audit (Returns Processing and Account Services)
Russell P. Martin, Director
Edward Gorman, Audit Manager
Gwendolyn Gilboy, Lead Auditor
Linda L. Bryant, Senior Auditor
Sharon Buford, Senior Auditor
Kathleen Hughes, Senior Auditor
Lawrence N. White, Senior Auditor
Denise Gladson, Auditor
Jonathan Lloyd, Auditor
Robert Carpenter, Information Technology Specialist
Martha Stewart, Information Technology Specialist

APPENDIX III. REPORT DISTRIBUTION LIST

Commissioner C
Office of the Commissioner – Attn: Chief of Staff C
Deputy Commissioner for Services and Enforcement SE

Deputy Commissioner, Wage and Investment Division SE:W

Director, Customer Account Services, Wage and Investment Division SE:W:CAS

Director, Accounts Management, Wage and Investment Division SE:W:CAS:AM

Director, Filing and Payment Compliance, Wage and Investment Division SE:W:CP:FPC

Director, Submission Processing, Wage and Investment Division SE:W:CAS:SP

Chief Counsel CC

National Taxpayer Advocate TA

Director, Office of Legislative Affairs CL:LA

Director, Office of Program Evaluation and Risk Analysis RAS:O

Office of Internal Control OS:CFO:CPIC:IC

Audit Liaison: Chief, Program Evaluation and Improvement, Wage and Investment Division

SE:W:S:PRA:PEI

APPENDIX IV. OUTCOME MEASURE

This appendix presents detailed information on the measurable impact that our recommended corrective actions will have on tax administration. This benefit will be incorporated into our Semiannual Report to Congress.

Type and Value of Outcome Measure

- Revenue Protection – Actual; $397,158. This amount is based on 350 ineligible individuals who were allowed to erroneously claim Residential Energy Credits on their tax returns (see page 6).

Methodology Used to Measure the Reported Benefit:

We used computer analysis to identify 362 individuals who were in prison or under the age needed to enter into a contract to purchase a residence and were allowed to erroneously claim these credits. Revenue Protection is comprised of 262 individuals in prison with a tax effect of $343,487 and 88 of

100 underage individuals with a tax effect of $53,671, with the remaining 12 underage individuals having no tax effect from the allowed Residential Energy Credits on their tax returns. Thus, the IRS erroneously allowed 350 (262 + 88 = 350) ineligible individuals to receive the benefit of Residential Energy Credits on their tax returns which lowered their tax by $397,158 ($343,487 + $53,671 = $397,158). Despite having the data available, the IRS did not develop a process to identify these individuals who filed tax returns erroneously claiming these credits.

APPENDIX V. RESIDENTIAL ENERGY CREDITS (FORM 5695)

Form **5695**

Department of the Treasury
Internal Revenue Service

Residential Energy Credits

▶ See instructions.
▶ Attach to Form 1040 or Form 1040NR.

OMB No. 1545-0074

2009

Attachment Sequence No. **158**

Name(s) shown on return | Your social security number

Before You Begin Part I: Figure the amount of any credit for the elderly or the disabled you are claiming.

Part I Nonbusiness Energy Property Credit (See instructions before completing this part.)

1	Were the qualified energy efficiency improvements or residential energy property costs for your main home located in the United States? (see instructions) ▶	1	☐ Yes ☐ No
	Caution: *If you checked the "No" box, you cannot claim the nonbusiness energy property credit. Do not complete Part I.*		
2	Qualified energy efficiency improvements (see instructions).		
a	Insulation material or system specifically and primarily designed to reduce the heat loss or gain of your home	2a	
b	Exterior windows (including certain storm windows) and skylights	2b	
c	Exterior doors (including certain storm doors)	2c	
d	Metal roof with appropriate pigmented coatings, or asphalt roof with appropriate cooling granules, that are specifically and primarily designed to reduce the heat gain of your home, and the roof meets or exceeds the Energy Star program requirements in effect at the time of purchase or installation	2d	
3	Residential energy property costs (see instructions).		
a	Energy-efficient building property	3a	
b	Qualified natural gas, propane, or oil furnace or hot water boiler	3b	
c	Advanced main air circulating fan used in a natural gas, propane, or oil furnace	3c	
4	Add lines 2a through 3c	4	
5	Multiply line 4 by 30% (.30)	5	
6	Maximum credit amount. (If you jointly occupied the home, see instructions)	6	$1,500
7	Enter the smaller amount of line 5 or line 6	7	
8	Enter the amount from Form 1040, line 46, or Form 1040NR, line 43 — 8		
9	Enter the total, if any, of your credits from Form 1040, lines 47 through 50, and Schedule R, line 24; or Form 1040NR, lines 44 through 46 — 9		
10	Subtract line 9 from line 8. If zero or less, **stop.** You cannot take the nonbusiness energy property credit	10	
11	**Nonbusiness energy property credit.** Enter the smaller of line 7 or line 10	11	

For Paperwork Reduction Act Notice, see instructions. Cat. No. 13540P Form **5695** (2009)

Form 5695 (2009) Page **2**

Before You Begin Part II:

Figure the amount of any of the following credits you are claiming.

- Credit for the elderly or the disabled.
- District of Columbia first-time homebuyer credit.
- Alternative motor vehicle credit.
- Qualified plug-in electric vehicle credit.
- Qualified plug-in electric drive motor vehicle credit.

Part II **Residential Energy Efficient Property Credit** (See instructions before completing this part.)

Note. *Skip lines 12 through 21 if you only have a* ***credit carryforward from 2008.***

12	Qualified solar electric property costs			12	
13	Qualified solar water heating property costs			13	
14	Qualified small wind energy property costs			14	
15	Qualified geothermal heat pump property costs			15	
16	Add lines 12 through 15			16	
17	Multiply line 16 by 30% (.30)			17	
18	Qualified fuel cell property costs	18			
19	Multiply line 18 by 30% (.30)	19			
20	Kilowatt capacity of property on line 18 above ▶ ______ x $1,000	20			
21	Enter the smaller of line 19 or line 20			21	
22	Credit carryforward from 2008. Enter the amount, if any, from your 2008 Form 5695, line 28			22	
23	Add lines 17, 21, and 22			23	
24	Enter the amount from Form 1040, line 46, or Form 1040NR, line 43	24			
25	**1040 filers:** Enter the total, if any, of your credits from Form 1040, lines 47 through 50; line 11 of this form; line 12 of the Line 11 worksheet in Pub. 972 (see instructions); Form 8396, line 11; Form 8839, line 18; Form 8859, line 11; Form 8834, line 22; Form 8910, line 21; Form 8936, line 14; and Schedule R, line 24. **1040NR filers:** Enter the amount, if any, from Form 1040NR, lines 44 through 46; line 11 of this form; line 12 of the Line 11 worksheet in Pub. 972 (see instructions); Form 8396, line 11; Form 8839, line 18; Form 8859, line 11; Form 8834, line 22; Form 8910, line 21; and Form 8936, line 14.	25			
26	Subtract line 25 from line 24. If zero or less, enter -0- here and on line 27			26	
27	**Residential energy efficient property credit.** Enter the smaller of line 23 or line 26			27	
28	Credit carryforward to 2010. If line 27 is less than line 23, subtract line 27 from line 23	28			

Part III **Current Year Residential Energy Credits**

29	Add lines 11 and 27. Enter the result here and on Form 1040, line 52, or Form 1040NR, line 48, and check box c on that line	29	

Form **5695** (2009)

End Notes

[1] Pub. L. No. 111-5, 123 Stat. 115 (2009).

[2] Equipment must be placed in service by December 31, 2016.

[3] The Credit amount for costs paid for a fuel cell system is limited to $500 for each one-half kilowatt of power capacity.

[4] Appendix V provides an example of Form 5695.

[5] *Verifying Eligibility for Certain New Tax Benefits Was a Challenge for the 2010 Filing Season* (Reference Number 2010-41-128, dated September 30, 2010).

[6] If a taxpayer and his or her spouse owned and lived apart in separate main homes, they may each qualify for

[7] Figure 3 illustrates the number of ineligible individuals for whom the IRS allowed erroneous Residential Energy Credits on their Tax Year 2009 tax returns. We subsequently evaluated the tax effect of the IRS allowing these erroneous Residential Energy Credits and determined that 350 of 362 ineligible individuals' taxes were lowered by $397,158 as a result. See Appendix IV for more details.

[8] To assess the reliability of the computer data processed through July 23, 2010, the TIGTA Office of Information Services validated the data that were extracted from IRS systems and we verified the accuracy of the data by comparing judgmental samples of data to the IRS information residing on the Integrated Data Retrieval System. The Integrated Data Retrieval System is an IRS computer system capable of retrieving or updating stored information; it works in conjunction with a taxpayer's account records.

[9] The Individual Master File contains general entity information for individual taxpayers such as name, address, and Social Security Number. The Individual Return Transaction File contains data transcribed from individual tax forms and accompanying schedules. The Individual Return Transaction File data were extracted from the IRS's mainframes and a run-to-run balancing was used, which involves documenting the records read in and written out at each step of the file processing to ensure all records were received and loaded.

[10] The Federal Bureau of Prisons and individual States voluntarily provide the IRS with the information for the Prisoner File, and the IRS receives most of the data to update the file in August and September. The TIGTA has previously reported concerns with the reliability of the data in the Prisoner File and, as such, our analysis is only as reliable as the data on which it is based.

[11] The National Account Profile contains IRS and Social Security Administration information for name control, date of birth, and date of death for each taxpayer identification number.

[12] Pub. L. No. 111-5, 123 Stat. 115 (2009).

[13] *Standards for Internal Control in the Federal Government* (GAO/AIMD-00-21.3.1).

INDEX

D

E

F

G

H

V

W